Sacramentals

Liturgical Symbols That Surround Us

JOHAN VAN PARYS

Imprimi Potest: Kevin Zubel, CSsR, Provincial
Denver Province, The Redemptorists

Published by Liguori Publications, Liguori, Missouri 63057
Liguori Publications, a nonprofit corporation, is an apostolate of the Redemptorists.
To learn more about the Redemptorists, visit Redemptorists.com.
To order, visit Liguori.org or call 800-325-9521

ISBN: 978-0-7648-2885-0
E-ISBN: 978-0-7648-7265-5

Library of Congress Cataloging-in-Publication Data
Names: Van Parys, Johan author
Title: Sacramentals : liturgical symbols that surround us / Johan van Parys.
Description: First edition. | Liguori, MO : The Queen's Work, Liguori Publications, [2025] | Includes index. | Summary: "A look at the meaning behind the primary elements of the sacraments of the Catholic Church as well as sacred objects, furnishings, images, and other items used in Catholic worship and devotions"-- Provided by publisher.
Identifiers: LCCN 2025039425 (print) | LCCN 2025039426 (ebook) | ISBN 9780764828850 paperback | ISBN 9780764872655 ebook
Subjects: LCSH: Sacramentals | Sacraments--Catholic Church | Christian art and symbolism
Classification: LCC BX2295 .V36 2025 (print) | LCC BX2295 (ebook)
LC record available at https://lccn.loc.gov/2025039425
LC ebook record available at https://lccn.loc.gov/2025039426

Printed in the United States of America
29 28 27 26 25 / 8 7 6 5 4
First edition

Cover design: Wendy Barnes

Liguori Publications has revived ***The Queen's Work*** imprint to support the needs of the people of God who desire a life of greater piety and devotion, and to encourage the positive spiritual energy that is present in the Church today.

Also available from Liguori Publications, ***Journey of Faith*** and ***Jornada de Fe*** are written in the engaging, pastoral style of the Redemptorists and speak clearly to audiences in their voice—adults, teens, children, and Hispanics. The program welcomes all generations and backgrounds to the Catholic faith, meeting the people where they are in their own faith journey. ***Journey of Faith*** and ***Jornada de Fe*** address relevant life issues, faith topics, and questions in a catechetical approach to OCIA/RICA.

CONTENTS

FOREWORD
TO THIS REVISED EDITION

Liguori Publications is pleased to offer *Sacramentals: Liturgical Symbols That Surround Us*. First published in 2012, this popular book helps lifelong Catholics and those preparing to enter the Church discover the fascinating meaning behind many of the objects, actions, prayers, and places that are part of our daily, liturgical, and sacramental lives.

Catholics are a sacramental people. We rely on signs and symbols, sacraments and sacramentals, to guide us on our journey of faith. Sacraments confer the grace of the Holy Spirit; sacramentals prepare us to receive it. In the sacraments, Christ shares his divine life with us, and sacramentals, through the prayer of the Church, bring us to holiness in Christ. Both sacraments and sacramentals draw their power from a single source—Christ. Through them, we are sanctified; in them, God is praised. (See *Catechism of the Catholic Church*, 1670.)

Johan van Parys, PhD, has expertly revised and expanded this edition to include an updated focus on the symbols and sacramentals that surround us and point us to the liturgy of the Church. (See *CCC* 1675.) May your faith life in Christ be enriched immensely by this informative and insightful presentation.

REV. THOMAS M. SANTA, CSSR
PRESIDENT / PUBLISHER LIGUORI PUBLICATIONS

FOREWORD FROM THE FIRST EDITION

Our lives are filled with symbols and symbolic acts, from the sign of the cross made on our forehead before we were baptized to the pall placed on our coffin at the end of our lives. In addition, between these two milestones in our lives as Christians, symbols surround us.

Some symbols are obvious and easily understood, such as the crucifixes many of us have in our homes. Others are more obscure and not as common, such as the moon under Mary's feet or the eagle at the side of St. John the Evangelist. Some symbols tell the stories of the saints, while others tell the story of our faith, and still others are essential parts of the liturgy and sacramental life of the Church. The latter are notable because the liturgy uses simple elements of our daily lives and turns them into life-altering worship symbols.

Symbols are very important in our daily and liturgical lives, so it is important to make sure we are familiar with them. To that end, Johan van Parys offers an excellent introduction to some of the most significant symbols in our lives.

The aim of *Sacramentals: Liturgical Symbols That Surround Us* is twofold. The book offers insight into our daily use of symbols and the symbolic acts that uniquely equip humans for the use of symbols in a religious context, as well as how our experiences with such simple elements as water, fire, bread, and wine prepare us for their sacramental use.

Dr. van Parys then talks about our daily use of symbols and our experiences of sacramental symbols on a human level, as in the primary sacramental symbols of baptismal waters, the Easter fire, and eucharistic bread and wine, as well as secondary symbols, such as the *Gospel Book*, a crucifix, or an altar table. Throughout, he offers opportunities to reflect on the meaning of these symbols and make further connections to our experiences of them.

The religious symbols discussed here are but a few of the many that surround us, but the groundwork the book lays encourages all of us to become more aware of and appreciate symbols on a deeper level. This understanding allows their impact to be even greater each time we encounter them in our lives of faith.

GIOVANNI CARDINAL LAJOLO
PRESIDENT EMERITUS OF THE GOVERNORSHIP OF VATICAN CITY STATE

INTRODUCTION

When I was a boy, I became very enamored of my great-aunt. At a young age, she left our hometown and moved to Brussels, the capital of Belgium, where she enjoyed a successful career and celebrated life to its fullest. She was beautiful, charming and captivating. Occasionally, she would invite me to enjoy dinner in her beautiful home and join her at the opera. Those were magical evenings—memories I cherish dearly.

Shortly after the death of her husband, she said goodbye to her glamorous life in Brussels and moved back to our small hometown, where she spent the rest of her life in a retirement community. Whenever I went back to Belgium, I visited her there. I remember those visits very well, especially our last visit. By then, my auntie suffered memory loss. As I knocked somewhat hesitantly on the door to her room and walked in, she smiled and nodded to invite me in. Though she had aged quite a bit, she looked radiant as always, dressed in a dark skirt and white blouse with her signature string of pearls around her neck. She was very pleasant and welcoming but clearly did not recognize me. I sat down across from her, and she immediately started telling random family stories. It was not always clear who she was talking about until she mentioned her sister: my grandmother. I quickly interrupted her and indicated that she was talking about my grandmother. Paying no attention to me, she continued with her stories. When she mentioned her favorite niece—my mom—I interrupted her again. Somewhat annoyed, she asked, "But who are you?" I told her I was Johan, her grandnephew. She retorted by informing me that Johan lived in the United States. "However," she said, "he is a nice boy. Whenever he comes to Belgium, he visits me."

IN A RELIGIOUS CONTEXT, SYMBOLS CREATE PATHWAYS AND OPEN PORTALS INTO THE MYSTERY OF OUR FAITH AND EVEN ALLOW US TO BECOME PART OF THE VERY MYSTERY WE CELEBRATE.

When it was time to leave, I asked if I could kiss her farewell. She agreed, and when I leaned in to kiss her cheek, tears were welling up in her eyes. She looked at me and whispered, "Sweet Johan, to think I did not recognize you." I cried with her. By the time I left, she had already forgotten who I was. That was the last time I saw her.

As I pondered our visit, I could not but delight in the power of non-verbal communication. Though I had tried to convince her I was her grandnephew, she only recognized me in what seemed a small gesture, a token of my love: a kiss on her cheek. In the end, no matter how hard I tried, it was not the words, but rather the gesture, that opened a portal into her mind.

This powerful experience with my aunt is exactly how non-verbal communication works. That which appears simple or ordinary can hold great meaning. And when we lack the words to express our deepest feelings and emotions, gestures have ways to communicate these feelings and emotions in ways words cannot. That is why we send flowers when someone has died or bring food when someone is ill. These gestures are often more eloquent than any words we could speak.

Symbols work in a similar, though more profound, way. In a religious context, symbols create pathways and open portals into the mystery of our faith and even allow us to become part of the very mystery we celebrate.

Although we may not always be aware of them, religious symbols surround us in our churches and even in our homes. They remind us of our faith and support us in our private and public prayer as we celebrate the sacraments and engage in personal devotions.

There are ten chapters in this book. The first chapter distinguishes between signs and symbols and between sacraments and sacramentals. The second chapter reflects on our human experience and the fundamental symbols that are used for the celebration of the liturgy: water, fire and light, oil, bread, and wine. The next two chapters look at the symbolic nature of the buildings in which we celebrate the liturgy and the symbolic contribution of the arts within them. The remaining chapters examine how liturgical furnishings, objects, vestments, and gestures function symbolically, concluding with considerations about the role of liturgical décor and sacred imagery. Each chapter ends with a set of questions intended to encourage individual or group reflection on the many symbols we encounter in our daily lives.

CHAPTER ONE

Signs and Symbols; Sacraments and Sacramentals

When we lack the words to express our feelings, we often use non-verbal modes of communication. We send flowers on various occasions, and certain flowers carry very specific meanings. Roses, especially red roses, are often presented as an expression of affection and love. That is why they are so popular on Valentine's Day. However, if the affection is not mutual, the same flowers can be experienced as annoying or even considered a form of stalking. A simple bouquet of roses has the power to evoke a strong emotional response of love or fear, even without an explanatory note. The flowers themselves communicate the message.

Though spoken language remains our principal tool of communication, we also communicate through our body language, through the way we dress, through signs we have established, and through symbols we have discovered. These powerful non-verbal ways of communicating are important in our daily lives as well as in the way we share our faith and celebrate our sacraments and sacramentals.

IN THE MOST SIMPLE OF TERMS, A SYMBOL IS SOMETHING THAT CAN BE PERCEIVED BY THE HUMAN SENSES WHILE CALLING FORTH ANOTHER REALITY THAT IS USUALLY IMMATERIAL, NOT CONCRETE, AND UNABLE TO BE SENSED.

Verbal Versus Non-Verbal Language

In our highly advanced society, people value verbal communication. We try to be careful and nuanced in what we say and how we say it. And, clearly, verbal communication sets people apart from other creatures and allows humans to communicate in much more complex ways. Yet, think of the difference between a conversation over the phone and a conversation that takes place in person, where we can read facial expressions and body language. The latter is often more enlightening than the former.

Our body language can help or hinder our communication with one another, often without our express knowledge. Some years ago, I was presenting a lecture to a group of undergraduates at the University of Notre Dame on the topic of eucharistic miracles. Although this was before the introduction of PowerPoint, I was well prepared with slides, music, and poetry. Yet, none of the information about medieval eucharistic miracles seemed of interest to the students. They slouched in their chairs, yawned, stared out the window, and didn't take a single note. Afterward, one of the students thanked me for an outstanding lecture. Although I heard his words, it was hard for me to believe him because of his slouching body language throughout my presentation. Though he said one thing, his body language communicated quite the opposite.

Body language is indeed quite powerful. A smile can imply joy at a reunion. Our tears reveal sorrow. A wink may disarm an otherwise tense situation with its playfulness.

When it comes to celebrating the liturgy, we are familiar with the different postures we take, such as genuflecting, blessing ourselves, kneeling, and the like. Yet, paying attention to our body language throughout the liturgy is of equal importance. Does our body language reflect respect and reverence for the sacrament we celebrate? Or does our body language communicate disinterest, boredom, or distraction? While this is particularly important for liturgical ministers, who are liturgical models, this also holds for the entire assembly.

Another form of intentional or unintentional non-verbal communication is the way we dress. When I was preparing to move to the United States, I was invited to a seminar on life in the United States held at the US Embassy in Brussels. One of the topics presented was on appropriate dress. The instructor suggested that people in the United States dress much more informally than Europeans. However, over the years, I have come to discover that there are different levels of informal dress. Informal dress appropriate for a baseball game is not the same as what might be worn for a company barbecue, while appropriate attire for the beach is different than what is worn for a run around the lake. Clothing indeed communicates much more than what the casual wearer might intend, even in the most informal setting.

This awareness of how clothing communicates becomes even clearer when we consider what is worn for more formal occasions. Most of us would not dream of wearing shorts, a rock-concert T-shirt, and flip flops to a funeral. Such an outfit fails to express the respect required by the occasion. Or, how confusing would it be if all women at a wedding wore long, white, elaborate gowns. Culture and custom dictate that only one woman wears white at a wedding, and that is the bride.

Clothes are also important for consecrated men and women, as they can be identified by what they wear. For example, Benedictines wear black habits, while Franciscans wear brown. Specific liturgical garb allows us to distinguish between deacons, priests, and bishops. And, for those of us in the assembly, does our attire reflect the reverence due to the sacrament we celebrate?

Signs and Symbols

Our world is filled with signs and symbols. Signs and symbols help us negotiate our daily lives and to co-exist with others, often without giving them much thought. We slow down and stop at a red light. We cross the street at a white-striped crosswalk. We give a heart-shaped box of chocolates on Valentine's Day. We exchange rings. We send flowers. We dip our fingers in Holy Water and make the sign of the cross. We light candles. We kneel in adoration. These are but a few of the many signs and symbols we encounter on a daily basis.

Signs and symbols differ from the spoken word in that they communicate a lot in little time. Think of a traffic light. No explanation is needed. When we see green, we move on. When we see yellow, we slow down. When we see red, we stop. Or, think of a time when a friend needed a hug. That hug was undoubtedly more eloquent than anything we could have said. There are so many instances in our lives in which we communicate more meaningfully through signs and symbols than with the spoken word. Signs and symbols are closely related, yet they are different.

The word "sign" comes from the Latin *signum,* which means "mark." Essentially, signs are simple images that convey specific information that is communally agreed upon. Signs tell us either to do something (such as to stop) or to refrain from doing something (such as to not make a left turn) very specific.

Signs can mean only one thing. There can be no confusion about the meaning of a sign. When we see a red circular sign with a white horizontal bar in the middle, we know not to enter. There may be words added to this sign, in languages we do not understand, but the sign's shape, color, and details (i.e., the white bar) have gained a universal understanding, which causes us to refrain from entering no matter where we are in the world.

For the most part, signs are chosen arbitrarily, and the connection between the sign and its meaning is largely random. There is neither a necessary nor a natural connection between the sign and its meaning. As a result, people must learn how to interpret the shapes and colors associated with different signs to learn their meanings. And the meaning of a sign stops at the sign itself. There is no meaning beyond the sign.

By contrast, symbols are never arbitrary. They are multifaceted and can convey multiple levels of meaning. They point to something beyond themselves. Symbols often speak to people on a pre-conscious level.

The word "symbol" is derived from the Greek prefix *syn-* and *ballein,* which means "to throw together, to bring together, or to connect." The origin of this term can be traced back to the Greek tradition of inscribing the names of friends onto fragments of pottery. When the friends had to leave one another, the shard would be broken, and each friend would take a piece. When they reunited, sometimes years later, their friendship was affirmed by the fact that the pieces came together. The bringing together of the tangible pieces of pottery symbolized the intangible friendship.

A symbol works in a similar manner, as it connects two different realities, a visible one and an invisible one, thus generating a meaning that is far beyond the visible reality. In the most simple of terms, a symbol is something that can be perceived by the human senses while calling forth another reality that is usually immaterial, not concrete, and unable to be sensed.

For symbols to work, there needs to be a connection between the human experience of the symbols and the deeper reality they symbolize. We are, for instance, able to make connections between water and baptism because the cleansing power of water helps us understand baptism as a symbol for divine cleansing. Our human experience of the destructive power of water helps us to connect baptism with our participation in the death of Jesus through baptism. The fact that water sustains life and life is born out of water also allows water to symbolize our new birth into the Church through the waters of baptism. Therefore, contrary to signs, symbols are never chosen arbitrarily. Symbols tap into our deeply rooted shared human experience with the symbols.

Symbols also require a specific context to work. Water does not always function as a symbol. It only becomes a symbol in a sacramental context. When we use water for washing dishes, the water is nothing but dishwater. When we use it for bathing, it is nothing but bath water. But when we use water for baptism, it becomes a symbol that holds great meaning. During the celebration of the sacrament, water is no longer ordinary; it becomes baptismal water that cleanses us from sin and drowns us in the death of Jesus so that we may rise with him again. Baptismal water is our entry into the Christian community. It births us into the Church. Thus, contrary to signs, symbols only work within a specific context.

Symbols are most often visual; however, symbols can also be olfactory, such as incense used during Mass. Symbols can be acoustical, such as church bells that call us to prayer. Symbols can be kinetic, such as processions or the washing of the feet on Holy Thursday.

Although there is some "learning" involved when relating to symbols, there is also an immediacy that allows us to connect more quickly and directly. When we place our hand on a hot stovetop, we do not carefully process what is happening before removing our hand.

Our reaction is direct and immediate. We remove our hand! Symbols, especially primary symbols, like water or fire, inspire a similar reaction. Symbols communicate immediately and directly, but not everything is communicated at once. That is the beauty of symbols. Like all good relationships, there is a fullness to their meaning that continues to deepen over time. We discover more levels of meaning as we continue to encounter a symbol.

This complexity of meaning is the main difference between signs and symbols. Signs need to be extremely simple and clear, while symbols enjoy a level of ambiguity. Signs communicate one message, while symbols create a greater meaning that leads to a deeper understanding. Signs are used when there is not enough time to communicate a message in words, as with traffic signs. Symbols are used when words cannot possibly suffice.

Daily Symbols and Sacred Symbols

When she was ten years old, one of my nieces proudly showed me her "promise ring." She went on to tell me about a boy in her class she liked very much. She understood that she was too young to date, but she was so pleased that he had given her this promise ring. When I asked her what the ring meant to her, she explained that the ring represented their promise to one another that one day they would get married.

I was moved by the innocence and even the naiveté of my niece, but I was also amazed at the layers of meaning that were heaped upon the simple string tied around her finger. In another context, this would be nothing but a simple string, yet in this context, it was much more. And though it was a far cry from any engagement diamond that might signify a future marriage, it was very important to her as a symbol of a lofty promise.

We are all surrounded by symbols and use them daily as we struggle to express the inexpressible marvel of the birth of a baby, the depth of our love when celebrating an anniversary, or the layers of deep emotions we experience when a loved one becomes ill or dies. In such situations, when we don't quite know what to say or when we fear our words fall short, we reach for symbols. Even when we look for a card to accompany flowers, the card itself becomes a symbol of our feelings, far beyond the preprinted wishes or any words we write by hand. The very act of giving the card becomes the symbol of care. Fundamentally, we are symbolic people, although we might not always be cognizant of this or aware of how we live out this reality in our daily lives.

When it comes to our faith, we use symbols even more readily to approach that which can neither be explained nor captured by words: the mysteries of creation and salvation. While science tries to explain certain aspects of these mysteries, symbols seek to reveal meaning as they invite us into an ever-deepening contemplation. The sacraments and sacramentals of the Catholic Church rely on symbols to evoke the mystery they reveal while at the same time

inviting us into that very mystery. This is the power of symbols.

Sacraments and Sacramentals

The word "sacrament" comes from the Latin *sacramentum*. It was borrowed by early Christian writers from its pre-Christian use in the Roman army, where it referred to the binding relationship between a soldier and his commander. This unbreakable relationship between the two was sealed by a *sacramentum* and consisted of an oath or pledge of fidelity sworn by the soldier to the commander. It also included a kind of branding on the soldier's body to indicate that he was bound to a particular commander until death. The Romans understood a *sacramentum* as both words and action that sealed a binding relationship that was sacred and could not be broken.

Tertullian, one of the great early Christian writers, who died around the year 220, borrowed this word when he described Christian initiation as a *sacramentum* that consisted of an oath, which in this case was the profession of faith and baptismal formula, and a branding that occurred through water and oil. Gradually, the term *sacramentum*, or "sacrament," came to refer to a great number of liturgical actions, including the Eucharist, ordinations, and consecrations.

Saint Augustine of Hippo (354–430) described a sacrament rather broadly as a "visible sign of an invisible grace" or, in Latin, *signia visibilia gratiae invisibilis*. He also held that a sacrament necessarily consisted of a material element (*elementum*) and a spoken word (*verbum*). Today, we refer to these two aspects of a sacrament as the "matter" of the sacrament (*elementum*) and the "form" of the sacrament (*verbum*). When the word, or form, joins the element, or matter, a sacrament is created (*accedit verbum ad elementum et fit sacramentum*). In terms of baptism, for example, the matter used is water, while the form is the formula pronounced during baptism: "I baptize you in the name of the Father, and of the Son, and of the Holy Spirit." When the formula is spoken while the water is poured, the sacrament is realized.

Although St. Augustine offers a foundational description of what a sacrament is, he did not narrow the number of sacraments to the seven we have today. That was still centuries away. As late as the beginning of the twelfth century, Hugh of St. Victor (ca.1100–1141) considered—in addition to the sacraments we know today—the blessing of holy water, the blessing of palms, the reception of ashes, bending the knee in prayer, monastic vows, saying the Creed, dedicating a church, and burial rites to be sacraments.

Peter Lombard (1100–1160) was one of the first to define the seven sacraments and to distinguish between sacraments and sacramentals. Based on Augustine's definition, Peter Lombard held that both sacraments and sacramentals are a "visible sign of an invisible grace." However, when it came to sacraments, he considered this definition to be too broad. A sacrament, according to Lombard, differs from a sacramental in that a sacramental is merely a *sign* of grace, whereas a sacrament is also a *cause* of grace. Since then, such sacred actions as blessing holy water, receiving ashes, genuflecting, taking religious vows, etc., are no longer considered to be sacraments but rather are known as sacramentals because although they are visible signs of God's grace, they are not causes of God's grace.

It was during Scholastic times (twelfth century) that the Catholic Church definitively established that there are seven sacraments: the sacraments of initiation (baptism, confirmation, and Eucharist), the sacraments of vocation (holy matrimony and holy orders), and the sacraments of healing (sacrament of the sick and reconciliation). The *Catechism of the Catholic Church* defines the sacrament as "efficacious signs of grace, instituted by Christ and entrusted to the Church, by which divine life is dispensed to us" (*CCC* 1131).

Both sacraments and sacramentals use visible signs, elements. Water, for instance, is used for the sacrament of baptism as well as for the sacramental of blessing with holy water. Our invisible God used visible signs to illuminate the mystery of the Divine because that which is visible and tangible is much more accessible to humans than that which is not.

The Use of Symbols in Sacraments and Sacramentals

Humans have the amazing capacity to be symbolic beings. Not only can we communicate with one another in a very literal manner, which already sets us apart from other life forms, but we can communicate in a symbolic manner, which distinguishes us even more. On Mother's Day, for instance, we not only congratulate our mothers, but we also give them hugs, cards, and flowers. On wedding anniversaries, we not only tell our spouses how much we love them, but we also offer chocolates and kisses as symbols of our love. Over time, these gifts have become symbols that enhance and underline our vows of love in a way that makes them more tangible. Even though flowers and chocolates are considered secondary in the hierarchy of symbols, they still are something tangible, which underlines that which is intangible: our love for one another.

Sacraments and sacramentals also make use of symbols, albeit primary symbols such as water, fire, oil, bread, and wine. These constitute the matter, or the "visible sign" of "invisible grace." Each of the seven sacraments has its own matter and thus its own symbol. The matter or symbol for the sacrament of baptism is water. Oil is used for confirmation, ordination, and the sacrament of the sick. And bread and wine are used for the celebration of the Eucharist.

These symbols are considered primary because humans intuitively relate to them due to our preternatural disposition to these primary symbols. Oil, for instance, is omnipresent in our lives. We use oil in our food; thus, it has a nourishing aspect. We use oil to soothe and heal our skin; thus, it has a healing aspect. Oil also harbors a very destructive power: the ability to explode or spread fire. Thus, oil can sustain life while, at the same time, it also can destroy life. Our human experience of oil allows it to communicate the many forms of God's salvific work in a person and in the Church when it is used in the sacraments of baptism, confirmation, holy orders, and the sacrament of the sick, as well as the consecration of altars and churches.

Faithful Reflections

We rely on many non-verbal elements of communication in our daily life, often without noticing it. These signs and symbols are an essential part of who we are. In worship, our instinctive and pre-symbolic relationship with primary symbols allows us to connect with the sacramental symbols that have become part of the liturgical richness of Christian gatherings throughout history. These non-verbal elements make up the "matter" for the celebration of the sacraments.

- ✠ *Think back to an important moment in your life, either of great joy or great sadness. What do you remember the most? Do you have any mementos of those moments? How do you treat those mementos?*
- ✠ *What are some symbols you have used to communicate with a loved one or shared with someone during times of sadness or joy or just because you wanted to do so?*
- ✠ *How have you experienced the power of symbols in the sacraments? What has been your favorite encounter?*

CHAPTER TWO

Primary Symbols as Liturgical Building Blocks

One of my favorite vacations was two weeks spent in Montana. We stayed in a very rustic cabin far away from any town and were surrounded by nature. We went to bed when it turned dark and got up as soon as the sun rose. We built fires in the fireplace to warm ourselves on chilly evenings, and we cooked meals on a wood stove. We drew water from the creek and swam in the lake. The wind blew on our faces as we walked through the fields. There were no buttons to push for ice, faucets for hot water, or switches for light or music. And there was no cellphone reception. Nothing was easy, but it was good to reconnect with the basic elements of earth: water, fire, air. These are the foundational building blocks of who we are and of the planet on which we live.

One afternoon as we were swimming in the lake, the sky turned black, winds swept over the water, and torrential rain came down. We struggled to get back to shore. The power of wind and water was evident in all its magnificence and terror. At that moment, I understood, more than ever before, why we use water for baptism. I had no problem imagining what it might be like to die and be buried in those churning waters.

IN THE MOST SIMPLE OF TERMS, A SYMBOL IS SOMETHING THAT CAN BE PERCEIVED BY THE HUMAN SENSES WHILE CALLING FORTH ANOTHER REALITY THAT IS USUALLY IMMATERIAL, NOT CONCRETE, AND UNABLE TO BE SENSED.

Water, like fire and food, is one of the primary symbols used in our liturgy. No matter where we live in the world, we have a profound connection to water. Those of us who live in a desert have a different relationship with water than those of us who live in flood-prone areas. Yet, all of us know how we depend on water, which at the same time has the power to destroy us. It is precisely because of our human dependence on water that these primary symbols constitute the perfect matter for the celebration of the sacraments. Biblical stories underscore our human experience with primary symbols. Just think of Noah and the flood, or Sodom and fire. Our shared human experience with primary symbols and their presence in Biblical narratives prepare us to relate to these symbols when they are used in the liturgy.

The Primary Symbol of Water

Our Pre-Symbolic Experience of Water

Although I have come to love being on or in the water, as a child, I was terrified of water. For the longest time, I blamed it on my swimming instructor. I was seven when I took my first swimming class. Not being the bravest, I hesitated to jump in. Noticing my hesitation, the instructor grabbed me and threw me into the deep end of the pool. I thrashed and spluttered, but I made it out of the water—upset but alive and afraid of water.

Although it made sense to attribute my fear to this one traumatic experience, I suspect the root of my fear goes much deeper and connects to our shared human experience of water. All of us relate to water in one way or another, whether we live in the swamps of Louisiana or the deserts of Nevada.

On the one hand, water is essential to all human life. Our bodies are made up of 90 percent water. We are conceived in water, and we are born out of water. We drink water. We use water to clean our homes and to cleanse ourselves. We relax while listening to water softly lapping on a riverbank, and we get exhilarated when surfing a towering wave in the ocean.

On the other hand, water is a powerful agent of destruction. Low-lying areas near the ocean are at risk of tsunamis, while rivers often flood the plains. Both experiences leave behind massive destruction and great human loss. However, the absence of water can also be destructive. A persistent drought parches crops and leads to cracked soil, the loss of food, the danger of fire, and the possible loss of life.

To summarize, we need water to survive, while that same water possesses the ability to destroy us. It is precisely these diverse and paradoxical human experiences with water that become pre-symbolic steppingstones for us to encounter water as a liturgical symbol, the matter of the sacrament of baptism.

Biblical References to Water

The Bible tells us of the power of water as a giver of life and an agent of destruction. Divine wrath is realized with water either against the chosen race or against an enemy. At the time of the great Flood, God allowed water to cover the whole earth: "Higher and higher on the earth the waters swelled, until all the highest mountains under the heavens were submerged. The waters swelled fifteen cubits higher than the submerged mountains. All creatures that moved on earth perished: birds, tame animals, wild animals, and all that teemed on the earth, as well as all humankind" (Genesis 7:19–21). In order to save the Israelites, God let the Egyptians be swallowed up by water: "Then Moses stretched out his hand over the sea; and the LORD drove back the sea with a strong east wind all night long and turned the sea into dry ground. The waters were split.... [A]t daybreak the sea returned to its normal flow...it covered...all Pharaoh's army... not even one escaped" (Exodus 14:21, 27–28).

Water is given to the Israelites by God to quench their thirst. When the Israelites were on their long journey through the desert on the way to the Promised Land, God provided them with manna to eat and water to drink: "Then, raising his hand, Moses struck the rock twice with his staff, and water came out in abundance, and the community and their livestock drank" (Numbers 20:11). The quenching of a more profound thirst is described by the prophet Isaiah when he writes how God invites all people to quench their thirst: "All you who are thirsty, come to the water!" (Isaiah 55:1).

In the Bible, water is also used on many occasions for cleaning and especially for ritual cleansing: "When they are about to enter the tent of meeting, they must wash with water, lest they die. Likewise, when they approach the altar to minister, to offer an oblation to the LORD, they must wash their hands and feet, lest they die" (Exodus 30:20–21).

Water, most importantly, is shown to be a place of revelation and a source of salvation: "I am baptizing you with water, for repentance, but the one who is coming after me... will baptize you with the Holy Spirit and fire"

(Matthew 3:11). Or, "The eunuch said, 'Look, there is water. What is to prevent my being baptized?'" (Acts 8:36).

Water in the Liturgy

Water is used in the sacramental, liturgical, and devotional life of the Church in a variety of ways. The most profound and life-altering use of water is in the sacrament of baptism. Our pre-symbolic experience of water as well as our biblical understanding prepare us well for the sacramental experience of baptism as bath, burial, and birth.

In the same way that water is used to wash our bodies, baptismal waters are used to cleanse our souls. Through their baptismal bath, the newly baptized—who are called neophytes, or "new shoots"—are washed from everything that stands between them and perfect union with God. Baptismal waters cleanse the neophytes from all personal sins as well as original sin.

Due to the potential of drowning in water, St. Paul aptly asked the Romans, "Or are you unaware that we who were baptized into Christ Jesus were baptized into his death?" (Romans 6:3). Baptismal waters then become the place of the neophytes' symbolic death with Christ.

Because water is absolutely necessary to sustain life, and because all life is conceived and born out of water, the baptismal font is the place where neophytes are born into the Church through the sacrament of baptism.

The Primary Symbol of Fire

Our Pre-Symbolic Human Experience of Fire

Since the beginning of human history, we have had a complex relationship with fire. Our ancient relatives treated fire with utmost deference and respect because they were neither able to create it nor control it. Once humans discovered ways to make fire and control it, our relationship with fire changed, and fire was used for cooking, protection, warmth, and any number of other uses. Nevertheless, even today, fire remains one of our best allies and is at the same time one of our fiercest adversaries.

Who does not love the crackling and dancing of fire in an outdoor fire pit? Throughout history, generations have sat around campfires

all over the world, telling stories and singing songs. Fire provides us with heat and light. We use fire to boil water and cook our meals, clear fields, and fertilize the soil. Reading a book beside a cozy fireplace during the dark of winter offers reprieve from the cold and warms our heart. Fire possesses many life-giving qualities.

On the other hand, fire has the power to destroy and kill. Forest fires devastate thousands upon thousands of acres of trees and plants each year, killing animals and sometimes people. The horror of a rushing brush fire or being trapped in a burning house is unimaginable. While fire helps us thrive and survive, it can threaten our very existence.

In summary, fire sustains life but also has the potential to destroy life. It is precisely this paradox which predestines fire and light as a primary liturgical symbol.

Biblical References to Fire

The Bible is filled with descriptions of how fire destroys, inspires, guides, and enlightens. Among the many stories of fire, some stand out; for example, the destructive power of fire is used by God to show anger and cause ruin: "The LORD rained down sulfur upon Sodom and Gomorrah, fire from the LORD out of heaven" (Genesis 19:24).

God used fire for a divine epiphany: "There the angel of the LORD appeared to [Moses] as fire flaming out of a bush. When he looked, although the bush was on fire, it was not being consumed" (Exodus 3:2).

God also used fire by night to guide the people: "The LORD preceded them, in the daytime by means of a column of cloud to show them the way, and at night by means of a column of fire to give them light. Thus they could travel both day and night" (Exodus 13:21).

Finally, God's spirit is manifested in fire that comes down on the apostles: "Then there appeared to them tongues as of fire, which parted and came to rest on each one of them" (Acts 2:3).

Fire in the Liturgy

Without question, the blessing of the Easter fire during the Easter Vigil on the night of Holy Saturday is the most striking example of liturgical use of fire. This liturgy uncharacteristically begins outside, as people gather around a (hopefully) substantial fire. As night sets, this fire offers warmth and light. It is good for people to arrive early so they can experience the fire. When the ministers arrive, the celebrant blesses the fire while evoking different qualities of fire:

O God, who through your Son
bestowed upon the faithful the fire of your glory,
sanctify + this fire, we pray,
and grant that,
by these Paschal celebrations,
we may be so enflamed with heavenly desire,
that with minds made pure
we may attain festivities of unending splendor.
Through Christ our Lord.

After preparing the paschal candle, the celebrant lights it from the Easter fire. Then, the candle is processed into a darkened church while the celebrant and the people light their individual candles from the paschal candle. Three times, the celebrant stops and announces, "The Light of Christ," and people respond, "Thanks be to God." After the third announcement, the darkened church is aflame with the candles held high by everyone present. Then, the Easter Proclamation or *Exultet* is sung, referencing "the glowing fire ignited for God's glory" and the one light "divided into many flames which are never dimmed."

While a large fire is only used once a year in the liturgy, candles are lit at all liturgical services. The primary candle is the Easter candle, or paschal candle, that is lit from the Easter fire and symbolizes the light of Christ that destroys all darkness.

Whether small or large, the flame of faith is kindled whenever candles or fire are used during liturgical celebrations. Sometimes, people light candles in religious shrines to symbolize their continued prayers to God. Candles are also lit at home as symbols of our ongoing prayer and devotion to God, Mary, and the saints. In all these settings, our pre-symbolic instincts are at work, drawing us to fire so our faith may be enkindled as we become wrapped in the power of symbol.

The Fundamental Symbol of Oil

Our Pre-Symbolic Human Experience of Oil

The olive tree is one of my favorite trees. Olive trees are extremely resilient. They have beautiful gnarled trunks and olive-green leaves, and they often enjoy long lifespans. Although they do not like the cold, they can withstand long droughts and live hundreds and even thousands of years. It is mind-boggling to think that some of the olive trees in the Garden of Olives where Jesus prayed the night before he died might still be standing as silent witnesses to the events that night.

Not only do I love olive trees, but, like millions of other people, I delight in their fruit. The smell of fresh virgin olive oil, cold or simmering in a pan, waiting for garlic to be added, is a delight for the senses. And who can resist the taste of good olive oil drizzled over beautiful tomato slices and basil leaves?

Of course, many kinds of vegetables provide oil. There are also animal oils and fossil fuels, such as petroleum. Some oils are prized for their culinary qualities, while others are used to soothe our skin when it cracks in the winter or burns in the summer. Scented oils provide sheen to our hair, perfume our bodies, and rouse our senses. Oil is also used to light lamps, fuel cars, and heat our homes. For better or for worse, oil has become an essential component of our daily lives.

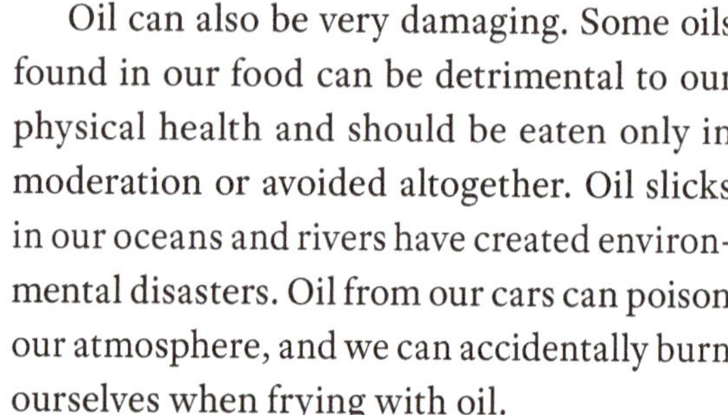

Oil can also be very damaging. Some oils found in our food can be detrimental to our physical health and should be eaten only in moderation or avoided altogether. Oil slicks in our oceans and rivers have created environmental disasters. Oil from our cars can poison our atmosphere, and we can accidentally burn ourselves when frying with oil.

Our pre-symbolic relationship with oil today is very complex and far removed from the simplicity that inspired early Christians to use it as a liturgical symbol. Nevertheless, when we are liberated from today's complexities, we still deeply connect to the experiences of the people of God in biblical times, when most of the oil came from the olive trees that still dot the Mediterranean and Middle Eastern landscapes.

Biblical References to Oil

Like other fundamental symbols, oil is used in multiple ways in the Bible. Oil first became a symbol of God's soothing and healing presence: "Therefore God, your God, has anointed you with the oil of gladness above your fellow kings. With myrrh, aloes, and cassia, your robes are fragrant. From ivory-paneled palaces, stringed instruments bring you joy" (Psalm 45:8–9). Or, "Then I bathed you with water, washed away your blood, and anointed you with oil" (Ezekiel 16:9).

Oil was also used to affirm God's presence with those who were appointed priest, prophet, and king. Aaron, for example, was anointed priest: "Then take the anointing oil and pour it on his head, and anoint [Aaron]" (Exodus 29:7). David was anointed as king: "Then Samuel, with the horn of oil in hand, anointed him in the midst of his brothers, and from that day on, the spirit of the LORD rushed upon David" (1 Samuel 16:13). Elisha was anointed as prophet: "You shall also anoint Jehu, son of Nimshi, as king of Israel, and Elisha, son of Shaphat of Abel-meholah, as prophet to succeed you" (1 Kings 19:16).

According to Scripture, people used oil in sacrifices, similar to their use of animal offerings: "Early the next morning Jacob took the stone that he had put under his head, set it up as a sacred pillar,* and poured oil on top of it" (Genesis 28:18). They also used oil to heal and soothe: "They drove out many demons, and they anointed with oil many who were sick and cured them" (Mark 6:13). Or, in the case of the Good Samaritan: "He approached the victim, poured oil and wine over his wounds and bandaged them" (Luke 10:34a). Finally, humans used oil to honor the body after death: "The women who had come from Galilee with him followed behind, and when they had seen the tomb and the way in which his body was laid in it, they returned and prepared spices and perfumed oils" (Luke 23:55–56a).

Oil in the Liturgy

Oil is used as matter, or a material aspect, in four of our seven sacraments: baptism, confirmation, ordination of priests and bishops, and the sacrament of the sick. Oil is also used for the dedication of altars and churches. These uses are patterned on both our pre-symbolic experience of oil and the biblical use of oil.

The permeating quality of oil symbolizes how the Spirit enters those who are being anointed and strengthens them for the task at hand, such as living the Christian life, in the

case of confirmation, or serving as a priest or bishop. The healing quality of oil provides an additional reason for its use in the anointing of the sick. The biblical use of oil in the anointing of priests, prophets, and kings also offers a theological foundation for its use in our sacraments.

Though the early church used only sacred chrism, today there are three different oils that are used in the sacramental life of the Church: 1) the oil of the catechumens for the baptism of infants and for adults preparing for initiation; 2) the oil of the sick for the anointing of the sick; and 3) sacred chrism for the baptism of infants, confirmation, holy orders, as well as the consecration of churches and altars.

The Fundamental Symbols of Bread and Wine

Our Pre-Symbolic Human Experience of Bread and Wine

When I was growing up, my maternal grandmother hosted weekly Sunday dinners for her children, their spouses, and their children.

These were great occasions for our extended family to get together and share our lives with one another while enjoying a lovely meal. In addition to the Sunday dinners, my immediate family shared meals together on a daily basis. Breakfast was somewhat on the run, but lunch and dinner were organized affairs where every member of our family sat together around the dining room table.

These Sunday dinners and weekday meals were always memorable, not only because of the food we shared but also because of our conversations and the time spent together. Looking back, I realize what a luxury it was to have had that time together and the resources to buy the food we were blessed to enjoy with one another. While our dining rituals were very important to me and the building block of our close-knit family, food and drink are also some of the most basic needs we have as human beings. Without them, we simply cannot survive. Today, many of us in the United States get our food nicely pre-packaged at the supermarket. This has removed us from the actual production of food. However, millions of people around the world are still reliant on what they can farm, gather, or hunt.

A staple for daily meals in many cultures around the world is bread in one form or another. In the United States, the bread aisle can be overwhelming with all the different kinds of bread that are offered, from basic sliced bread to luxurious baked loaves for festive occasions. Though the act of breaking bread is often abandoned in favor of buying sliced bread, breaking bread still lingers in our common memory. Whole loaves can easily be found in bakeries, and the temptation to break off a piece of a freshly baked baguette is very real.

The drinking of wine is also a centuries-long part of many cultures. Wine has been ascribed medicinal qualities, as it was used to settle upset stomachs or to clean wounds. Still, the principal quality of wine is to add festivity to a gathering and emphasize unity among those who share the cup. Although current practices dictate that each guest has his or her own glass at dinner parties, this was not always the case. The custom of sharing a common cup among table guests has a long history as part of sharing meals together and at other gatherings.

Because of our deep pre-symbolic connection with breaking bread and sharing wine, the connection to the sacramental and symbolic use of bread and wine can easily be made.

Biblical References to Food

The Bible uses bread in many contexts, from basic food to ritual food to spiritual nourishment. In the Hebrew Scriptures, bread is offered to guests as a sign of hospitality: "He urged them so strongly, however, that they... entered his house. He prepared a banquet for them, baking unleavened bread, and they dined" (Genesis 19:3). Unleavened bread is

used in rituals and as a sign of the covenant between God's people and the people of Israel: "For seven days you must eat unleavened bread. From the very first day you will have your houses clear of all leaven. For whoever eats leavened bread from the first day to the seventh will be cut off from Israel" (Exodus 12:15).

In the New Testament, Jesus used bread to describe several different realities. When he taught his disciples to pray the one perfect prayer, he included a petition to "Give us today our daily bread" (Matthew 6:11). In this instance, bread refers to all earthly food. Through the miracle of the multiplication of the loaves and fishes, Jesus revealed himself as the Son of God. (See John 6:11–13.) Jesus also used bread in explaining to his disciples that he is our spiritual food for eternal life when he stated, "I am the living bread that came down from heaven; whoever eats this bread will live forever; and the bread that I will give is my flesh for the life of the world" (John 6:51). Finally, he used bread to refer to his self-sacrifice when, after blessing and breaking the bread, he said, "Take and eat; this is my body" (Matthew 26:26).

Saint Paul used bread when he spoke about the unity of the Church, the body of Christ: "Because the loaf of bread is one, we, though many, are one body, for we all partake of the one loaf" (1 Corinthians: 10:17).

Though there are many reprimands against drinking too much wine in the Hebrew Scriptures, there are also many references to wine as celebration: "You make the grass grow for the cattle and plants for people's work to bring forth food from the earth, wine to gladden their hearts, oil to make their faces shine, and bread to sustain the human heart" (Psalm 104:14–15). And, "Go, eat your bread with joy and drink your wine with a merry heart, because it is now that God favors your works" (Ecclesiastes 9:7). Sometimes, wine is used in reference to the heavenly banquet: "On this mountain the LORD of hosts will provide for all peoples a feast of rich food and choice wines, juicy, rich food and pure, choice wines" (Isaiah 25:6).

In the New Testament, Jesus changed water into wine at the wedding at Cana. This was his first miracle by which he revealed himself as the Son of God: "Jesus did this as the beginning of his signs* in Cana in Galilee and so revealed his glory, and his disciples began to believe in him" (John 2:11). Most importantly, Jesus used wine at the Last Supper as the symbol of his very own blood that he would shed for our salvation: "Then he took a cup, gave thanks, and gave it to them, saying, 'Drink from it, all of you, for this is my blood of the covenant, which will be shed on behalf of many for the forgiveness of sins'" (Matthew 26:27–28).

In his writings, St. Paul uses many occasions to affirm the truth that when we drink from the eucharistic cup, we share in the Blood of

Christ: "The cup of blessing that we bless, is it not a participation in the Blood of Christ? The bread that we break, is it not a participation in the Body of Christ?" (1 Corinthians 10:16). Or, in the extended narration of the Last Supper: "For I received from the Lord what I also handed on to you, that the Lord Jesus, on the night he was handed over, took bread, and, after he had given thanks, broke it and said, 'This is my body that is for you. Do this in remembrance of me.' In the same way also the cup, after supper, saying, 'This cup is the new covenant in my blood. Do this, as often as you drink it, in remembrance of me.' For as often as you eat this bread and drink the cup, you proclaim the death of the Lord until he comes. Therefore whoever eats the bread or drinks the cup of the Lord unworthily will have to answer for the body and blood of the Lord" (1 Corinthians 11:23–27).

Bread and Wine in the Liturgy

Bread and wine are used for the celebration of the sacrament of the Eucharist, which is both the culmination of the sacraments of initiation and a sacrament that we celebrate as weekly and sometimes daily nourishment on our earthly journey of faith.

After discerning and preparing to become a full member in the Church, those who have celebrated the sacraments of baptism and confirmation are welcomed to the table of the Lord. In the same way that a family table symbolizes unity among all those seated around it, the altar table in the church is reserved for those who are members of the community. However, the altar table symbolizes not only unity among those gathered around it but also the sacrifice Jesus made for us, as well as our willingness to face the same sacrifice if we are asked to do so.

Faithful Reflections

God's presence is so extravagant that it flows through nature, our daily lives, and the faith and rituals we share. We can connect with the fundamental liturgical symbols of water, fire, light, oil, bread, and wine because we use them in our daily lives. These pre-symbolic experiences stay with us as we read about these symbols in Scripture and experience them in our worship. While we can learn more about the meaning of symbols by reading about them, we might do well to immerse ourselves in the elements at hand. What would it be like to set aside some time each week to experience water in a new way, light a candle during our prayer at home, rub oil on our skin, break bread rather than slice it, and toast God's presence with good wine?

✠ *How do you relate to water? What do you think about when you bless yourself upon entering the church?*

✠ *What is your strongest memory of fire or light? How does that impact your experience of fire and light in the liturgy?*

✠ *What liturgical symbol is most meaningful to you? What makes it so? What symbol would you like to become more meaningful? How might that happen?*

CHAPTER THREE

The Symbolic Meaning of Sacred Architecture

On October 28, 1944, Winston Churchill gave a now-famous speech during the rebuilding of the House of Commons after World War II. In it, he solemnly stated, "We shape our dwellings, and afterward our dwellings shape us." In 1960, *Time* magazine translated this phrase as, "We shape our buildings; thereafter they shape us." This idea has remained powerfully present in modern-day thinking about architecture. Although we design and build all our buildings, be they public or private, sacred or secular, they, in turn, shape us once they are built. Not only do they shape the people who built them, but they continue to impact successive generations.

Should we think that church buildings express only the theology of a certain age and enable the liturgy of a certain time, we would underestimate their formidable ability. Cathedrals, churches, and chapels continue to impress their meaning and convey the liturgical theology for which they were built long after that age and time have passed.

We can see this dynamic present in the architecture of Saint Peter's Basilica in Rome. This important church was built to honor St. Peter, first among the apostles and martyr for the faith. Emperor Constantine erected the original Basilica of Saint Peter in the fourth century above what was believed to be Peter's tomb. By the end of the fifteenth century, however, the Constantinian basilica had fallen into disrepair, and its architectural style was so outdated that a new basilica was built. Planning began in 1505, and the Basilica of Saint Peter as we know it today was completed in 1625. Among the successive architects were Bramante, Michelangelo, and Maderno.

Though visitors might not realize it, the architecture of Saint Peter's directs them to the main altar erected above St. Peter's tomb. This trajectory begins at the plaza in front of Saint Peter's Basilica, where Gian Lorenzo Bernini's colonnade draws all who enter the plaza into a mystical journey toward the tomb of St. Peter. Monumental stairs lead from the piazza to the grand portico of the basilica, where majestic bronze doors open into the nave. Once we are inside, our eyes are drawn along the center aisle to the bronze baldachin, or canopy, designed by Bernini and built right above the tomb of St. Peter. Even visitors who do not realize that St. Peter is buried there are still visually guided to that very place. Indeed, we shape our architecture, and, in turn, it shapes and guides us.

THE ORIGINS OF CHRISTIAN ARCHITECTURE ARE QUITE SIMPLE AND MODEST—TYPICAL FOR A NEWLY ESTABLISHED RELIGION THAT WAS STILL FINDING ITS WAY AND WAS NOT UNIVERSALLY ACCEPTED.

A Brief History of Church Architecture

For some 2,000 years, Christians have built cathedrals, churches, and chapels that express our faith, serve our liturgy, and inspire devotion. The result is a history of church architecture that is both impressive and complex. It is impressive because it gives us a collection of buildings and art of unparalleled beauty. It is complex because it is the result of an ongoing search for the best possible way to house the faithful as they pray, grow in their faith, and live as the body of Christ in a very specific time and place.

In a way, church architecture could be called a work in progress. It reveres its rich past and learns from it. It seeks to be informed by the present. And it looks toward the future with great hope and anticipation. Church architecture in every age is the result of an ongoing dialogue between architecture and art, faith and worship, and the world in which we live. This relationship is at times freeing because of the support and wider expression of faith that is welcomed by the Church, and it is at times restricting, as the Church varies between fostering new expressions of church art and architecture and prescribing strict directives for the construction and decoration of churches.

The origins of Christian architecture are quite simple and modest—typical for a newly established religion that was still finding its way and was not universally accepted. The first Christians, who were born Jewish, continued to pray in Jewish synagogues and gathered in private homes. They baptized where there was water, be that outside in a stream or in public baths. These existing types of architecture merely provided a temporary shelter for Christians at worship rather than being a place of prayer to call their own. As the Christian communities grew, certain houses were designated as so-called house-churches, which were adapted to accommodate worship, including baptism, and other Church needs. Some good examples of these house-churches can be found in Dura-Europos (235 CE), as well as in Rome, where a third-century house-church known as the *Titulus Equitii* can be found under the sixth-century Church of San Martino ai Monti, though scholars do not agree on the latter.

After years of persecution, Christianity was finally ratified in 313 by Emperor Constantine through the Edict of Milan. In 380, Emperor Theodosius solidified the place of Christianity by making it the official religion of the Roman Empire. As a result, Christianity grew exponentially, and worship was allowed to happen in public places. This change drastically impacted Christian liturgy and the buildings that housed it. It was no longer sufficient for architecture to simply shelter and accommodate the liturgy. Buildings needed to make a theological and even political statement. From that moment, Christians began to use the formative power of architecture very effectively to express their

faith and to house their worship. The Constantinian basilicas, such as the first Saint Peter's Basilica; the Carolinian and Romanesque churches; the great Gothic cathedrals; and the magnificent Renaissance, Baroque, and Rococo churches all have their own history and very specific liturgical and theological—and sometimes political—messages that they have conveyed for centuries and still impress upon those who enter them today, despite vast changes in theology and liturgical styles.

The development of successive architectural styles and forms that had evolved over the centuries came to a halt in the nineteenth and early twentieth centuries, when Church architects fell back on previous architectural styles and forms. The ensuing Byzantine, Romanesque, and Gothic revival churches all illustrate a yearning for a Church, a theology, and a liturgy of the past. The imitation of known architectural styles was a reaction to the devastating impact Catholicism had experienced due to such dramatic moments in European history as the French Revolution. Being at a loss for their own meaning system, they borrowed from the glorious Christian past and adopted architectural expressions that held enough theological meaning to carry past forms into the future.

Since the middle of the twentieth century, liturgists and architects alike have engaged in a search for a true revival. This revival was not merely one of style, but of essential Christian truths that were translated into common languages, expressed in authentic liturgy, and celebrated in meaningful buildings. This fascinating journey has produced churches that may be different in material, style, and scope, but they share similar areas, such as the gathering place, the place for baptism, the place for the celebration of the Eucharist, the place for the reservation of the Eucharist, the place for reconciliation, and the sacristy.

Sacred Architecture and Sacred Style?

Contrary to some people's wishes, the Catholic Church has never exclusively embraced any specific style when it comes to architecture and art. On the contrary, the Catholic Church has always welcomed innovative styles and the most up-to-date techniques. Not only does the history of Catholic architecture illustrate a great variety of styles and tastes in church art and architecture, but official Church documents also support and even encourage the use of the artistic genius of every age, especially after the Second Vatican Council. *Sacrosanctum Concilium*, the document on the liturgy promulgated by Pope Paul VI during the Second Vatican Council, states, "The Church has not adopted any particular style of art as its very own but has admitted styles from every period, according to the proper genius and circumstances of peoples and the requirements of the many different rites in the Church.... In this way, contemporary art can add its own voice to that wonderful chorus of praise sung by the great masters of past ages."

Pope St. John Paul II echoed this opinion

in *The General Instruction of the Roman Missal* (*GIRM*) from 2002, where it is stated, "The Church constantly seeks the noble assistance of the arts and admits the artistic expressions of all peoples and regions. In fact, just as she is intent on preserving the works of art and the artistic treasures handed down from past centuries and, in as far as necessary, on adapting them to new needs, so also she strives to promote new works of art that are in harmony with the character of each successive age."

The document on *Inculturation and the Roman Liturgy* states that "art in the church, which is made up of all peoples and nations, should enjoy the freedom of expression as long as it enhances the beauty of the buildings and liturgical rites, investing them with the respect and honor which is their due.... The same applies to the shape, location, and decoration of the altar, the place for the proclamation of the word of God, and for baptism, all the liturgical furnishings, vessels, vestments, and colors. Preference should be given to materials, forms, and colors that are in use in the country."

To ensure that the liturgy is celebrated in the most appropriate manner for a given time and place, and to guarantee that the art effectively conveys the Christian message, the Catholic Church grants artists considerable freedom to create art that resonates with individuals living in that specific context. This does not mean, however, that the art of ages past or from other locations is necessarily unsuitable. On the contrary, every work of art ever made in service of the mission of the Church remains part of the great repository of sacred art. And should one be tempted to relegate art of the past to pious attics or stuffy museums, it is good to remember that all sacred art remains laden with the Christian message and retains the ability to speak to people.

The Place for Gathering

The gathering space serves as a transitional area from the secular world to the sacred domain. Parishioners arrive for worship from their residences, workplaces, or vacation cabins and possibly have not seen one another for a week. Many events may have transpired during that time, prompting them to share stories about their lives, offer consolation in moments of sorrow, and express hopes for the future. They may not be immediately ready to quiet down and prepare for the liturgical celebration. The gathering space facilitates the transition from home to church, from daily activities to the celebration of the liturgy, and from the profane to the sacred. This transition is often challenging and begins when individuals prepare for church, continues through their drive or ride to church, the parking lot experience, and the walk to the church—whether it is wet, windy, hot, or icy—and culminates in the gathering space before entering the church proper.

Historically, church buildings have always had some sort of transitional space to accommodate the segue from the profane to the sacred. The great Mediterranean basilicas of the fourth century had large courtyards, often with fountains that allowed for some washing up and elaborate cloisters that provided shelter from sun and rain. The celebrated Romanesque and Gothic cathedrals had vast plazas and a narthex to accommodate transitional encounters and conversations. Many contemporary churches have a dedicated space for gathering and transitioning to avoid an all-too-abrupt segue from the profane to the sacred. In some of these newer churches, the baptismal font is in the gathering space, symbolizing that in the sacrament of baptism, we transition from our pre-Christian life to our participation in the body of Christ.

The Place for the Assembly

When the body of Christ gathers for worship, we do so according to our different roles in the liturgical assembly. Those fulfilling these different roles do so from very specific places in the church building. A lector proclaims the Word of God from the ambo. The celebrant presides over the Eucharist from the sanctuary. A baptism happens in the baptistery. The choir sings from the choir loft or from another designated space specific to their ministry. And the nave, or the body of the church, is the place designated for the assembly at worship. The word "nave" comes from the Latin *navis*, which means "ship." This might be because the nave of a church is reminiscent of the hull of a ship. It might be a reference to the ark of Noah that saved humanity. The "ship of the church" or the "barque of Saint Peter" is also a symbol used for the church because the church is a safe ship that allows us to navigate the turbulent waters of life.

Though seating arrangement in some churches may belie this basic principle, the place of the assembly in a church serves a very different purpose compared to the place for the audience in a theater. Typically, theater audiences do not engage in the performance, except in certain interactive theatrical productions. By contrast, the assembly is to participate fully, actively, and consciously in the celebration of the liturgy. Therefore, sightlines and acoustics are of the utmost importance for the optimal functionality of the nave. The nave also needs to accommodate the liturgical postures of the assembly as they stand, sit, and kneel. In addition, the nave needs to encourage the assembly's sung and spoken word as they lift their hearts in prayer.

The place of the assembly is also where several ritual actions—such as the many processions that are part of our liturgies—take place. Sometimes, these processions involve only a few people, but, on a few occasions, such as on Palm Sunday of Our Lord's Passion and during the Easter Vigil, the procession involves the entire assembly. The Communion procession at Mass also involves the better part of the assembly. Several processions happen only during specific liturgies, such as the procession to the baptismal font during baptism, the procession of the wedding party during the celebration of holy matrimony, and the procession with the coffin or urn at funerals. The nave needs to accommodate these processions and more.

Because the nave is often the place where devotional chapels are located, it is the place where the devotional life of the Church—such as Stations of the Cross, Mary crownings, and devotions to the saints—unfolds.

Provisions should also be made for people who use walkers and wheelchairs. This means that the aisles should be wide enough while seating should be flexible to accommodate wheelchairs. Hearing devices and a location for an American Sign Language interpreter should be planned for those who are hard of hearing. Mass leaflets in Braille could be made available for those who live with visual impairment.

The Place for Baptism

Baptism is the first of the seven sacraments of the Catholic Church. It is the sacrament that incorporates us into the body of Christ, the Church, and it is the entryway to the other sacraments. The main characteristics of baptism can be understood through these three images: baptismal bath, baptismal burial, and baptismal birth. In baptism, we are washed clean from everything that prevents perfect union with God, who claims us as adopted children. In baptism, we are buried with Christ so that we may rise with him on the last day. In the waters of baptism, we are birthed into the Church, the body of Christ.

Early Christians baptized wherever they could find water, preferably moving water, such as in rivers. After Christianity became one of the accepted religions in the Roman Empire (313 CE), bigger places for baptism were required because of the great number of conversions. At first, popular Roman public baths were used for baptism. These public baths inspired the construction of proper baptisteries, which were built exclusively to house the sacrament of baptism, thus emphasizing the importance of this sacrament.

The first baptisteries were large buildings with elaborate decorations and baptismal pools that allowed for the full immersion of adults. These baptismal pools came in different shapes, each in their own way illustrating the theological truth that in baptism we die with Christ to rise with him on the last day. Some fonts were octagonal, or eight-sided, referencing the eighth day: the day of the resurrection. Other fonts were hexagonal in shape, or six-sided, referencing the sixth day, or the day of Jesus' death. Others were cruciform or shaped

like tombs. Only cathedrals had baptisteries because the sacraments of initiation were celebrated by the bishop.

By the sixth to seventh centuries, several important shifts had taken place. First, Christianity, which had mostly been a city religion, spread to the countryside, and bishops sent priests to minster to the people there. Second, Christianity had become so popular that most adults had been baptized, leaving only infants to be baptized. Third, the doctrine of original sin caused parents to have their children baptized as soon as possible after birth due to the high child mortality rate and out of fear of eternal damnation. As a result, baptism was detached from the other two sacraments of initiation (confirmation and eucharist) and was no longer celebrated by the bishop alone, but also by priests. In the West, confirmation continued to be the prerogative of bishops, who administered the sacrament wherever they could, no matter the age of the confirmand.

At the same time, a greater emphasis was placed on the effect of the sacrament rather than on the way the sacrament was celebrated. Thus, the custom of immersion disappeared and was replaced with the pouring of a little bit of water on the child's head. Though still valid, this manner of baptizing gradually eroded the full experience of the sacrament and in turn had a great impact on the place for baptism. Separate baptisteries fell out of favor and were reduced to small baptismal chapels inside the churches. Large immersion fonts were replaced with small pedestal fonts used for affusion rather than immersion. Out of fear that holy water might be stolen for witchcraft, the baptismal chapels had lockable gates, while the small pedestal fonts were covered and locked. Soon, artists and artisans saw this as an opportunity to create elaborate covers for these fonts. As a result, the water, which is the primary and foundational symbol used for baptism, was reduced to what fit in the ever-shrinking pedestal font, inaccessible due to the locked gates of the baptismal chapel, and hidden from view by the covers over the fonts.

Following the Second Vatican Council, the

Catholic Church rediscovered how baptism was celebrated in early Christian communities and reintroduced several of those practices. The fact that more and more unbaptized adults were seeking the sacraments of initiation was a great impetus for this. The Rite of Christian Initiation of Adults, now known as the Order of Christian Initiation of Adults, which had been lost in favor of infant baptism, was re-instituted. Baptism by immersion again became the norm and is to be done preferably in the presence of the community, because it is by virtue of baptism that the neophytes, or newly baptized, become members of the body of Christ. Since then, the place for baptism has regained its place of importance and is visible to the entire assembly in many contemporary or renovated churches. In addition, many new fonts are larger in size to allow for immersion of adults. As had been the case in the past, they again come in many different shapes, illustrating the theology of baptism. And the water, the primary symbol of baptism, is again visible and accessible. When entering a church, we can walk to the baptismal font, bless ourselves, and remind ourselves of our baptismal promises in the place where they were made, either by ourselves or by our parents.

The Place for the Celebration of the Eucharist

The Eucharist is the third of the three sacraments of initiation. By contrast to baptism and confirmation, which can only be celebrated once, the Eucharist can and should be repeated. This is why the entire body of Christ, the Church, gathers each Sunday to celebrate the Eucharist. The Eucharist comprises two main parts: the Liturgy of the Word and the Liturgy of the Eucharist. In the Liturgy of the Word, we are nourished by the word of God that is proclaimed and that is elucidated during the homily. In the Liturgy of the Eucharist, we do what Jesus told us to do during the Last Supper as we share in his sacred Body and Blood.

The assembly, the different ministers, and the two essential parts of the Eucharist inform how the building that accommodates this celebration should be designed. First and foremost, the building needs to accommodate the full, active, and conscious participation in the celebration of the Eucharist by all who are present. As mentioned, this means that the space needs to allow for the entire assembly to see and hear the distinctive parts of the eucharistic celebration. The space also needs to accommodate the different ritual postures, such as kneeling, standing, sitting, and processing.

Some members of the community—such as the celebrant, deacons, lectors, psalmist, and servers—have specific and distinct liturgical roles. A distinct place is reserved for them so they may exercise their ministries as well as possible. This specific area is referred to as the sanctuary, which comes from the Latin word *sanctus,* meaning "holy." In the past, the sanctuary was strictly reserved for ordained minsters and altar servers. The Communion rail, which divided the sanctuary from the nave of the church, was the demarcation line. Today, anyone who has a ministerial role that requires access to the sanctuary is welcome to enter the sanctuary. Incidentally, some Christian denominations refer to the entire worship space as the sanctuary.

The sanctuary in many Catholic churches is raised and houses some of the principal liturgical furnishings. Of all liturgical furnishings, the altar is of the highest importance. It is at the altar that the sacrifice of the Mass is celebrated. For that reason, the altar itself is a symbol of Christ. That is why the altar is properly vested. That is why the ordained ministers reverence the altar at the beginning and end of Mass and incense the altar during the opening procession and at the preparation of the altar and gifts. And that is why all ministers bow every time they pass by the altar.

The ambo, sometimes referred to as lectern, is the place from where the word of God is proclaimed by the lectors, the deacon, and/or the priest. Unlike the altar, the ambo is merely a place for proclamation and, as such, is not a symbol of Christ. The *Gospel Book,* containing the word of God, however, is considered a symbol of Christ. That is why the *Gospel Book* is processed into the church by the deacon or, in his absence, a lector. That is why the *Gospel Book* is honored with incense before the proclamation of the gospel and kissed by the deacon or priest after the proclamation. And that is why the *Gospel Book* is brought to the bishop, so he may kiss it and bless the people.

The chairs for the celebrant and the deacon, and, in the case of a cathedral, the chair for the bishop, or the cathedra, are also present in the sanctuary. By their size, material, and style, they should illustrate the role these men have in the community both during and after the liturgy. However, they should also speak to the humility that is a characteristic of the ministers of Christ.

The tabernacle that houses the Blessed Sacrament is sometimes located in the sanctuary. This is especially the case in older churches, where the tabernacle is part of the high altar. Other churches may have a special chapel dedicated to reserve the Blessed Sacrament, so the tabernacle will be located there.

The Place for the Reservation of the Eucharist

During the first centuries of the Church, the Blessed Sacrament was primarily reserved for Communion of the sick, especially those who were dying. It was believed that no one should make the great journey of faith to the next life without having been nourished by the Body

of Christ, the food for the journey, viaticum. There was no common or prescribed place for reservation during these first centuries, except that it had to be done with respect. The Blessed Sacrament may have been reserved in the home where the priest lived or in one of the rooms adjacent to the church. What is certain is that the Blessed Sacrament was not reserved in the main body of the church.

The manner of reservation was also quite diverse. The earliest containers for reservation may have been simple wooden boxes. These became more complex as time went on, and by the tenth century, the most popular type of container was in the shape of a dove, and it hung in the sanctuary. Another common shape was that of a tower, known as the sacrament tower, which was located in or near the sanctuary.

Not until after the Council of Trent, in the mid-sixteenth century, did the custom of reserving the Eucharist in the middle of the high altar became popular. Although this practice was encouraged, older churches preserved the tradition of reserving it in a special chapel behind the apse or in a side chapel. This is still the practice in many cathedrals in Europe, including Saint Peter's Basilica in Rome, where the Blessed Sacrament is reserved in a separate chapel to the side of the nave.

In the United States, most churches that were built before Vatican II have a tabernacle on the main altar which is in the apse of the church. Churches that were built after the Second Vatican Council or those that have been renovated since then, often have a special chapel that has been designed for the reservation of the Blessed Sacrament. These chapels are designed to accommodate prayer before the Blessed Sacrament, either reserved in the tabernacle or exposed in the monstrance.

The General Instruction of the Roman Missal (*GIRM*) calls for the Eucharist to be reserved in accordance with the structure of each church and legitimate local custom in a "tabernacle in a part of the church that is truly noble, prominent, conspicuous, worthily decorated, and suitable for prayer." The Eucharist should not be reserved on the altar that is used for the celebration of the Eucharist, however, and only one tabernacle should be present in each church. The tabernacle may be placed either in the main sanctuary or in a chapel that is suitable for adoration and the private prayer of the faithful that is integrally connected with the church and is conspicuous to the faithful" (*GIRM* 314–317).

The Place for Reconciliation

Before the Second Vatican Council, the sacrament of reconciliation was known as confession. The latter emphasized the act of confessing sins, while the former emphasizes the experience of healing and reconciliation with God and with the Church that takes place in this sacrament.

Typically, confession took place in confessionals. These were set up in such a way that the identity of the person confessing their sins was protected. In many churches, the confessional accommodated one person kneeling on either side of the priest so that when one person confessed on one side, the next in line could get ready on the other side to do the same. Depending on the size of the church, two or more confessionals flanked the nave. Many older churches have preserved their original confessionals because of their historical or artistic value. However, in most cases, these are no longer used.

Today, the place for reconciliation is known as the reconciliation chapel rather than a confessional. These chapels are less intimidating than confessionals and emphasize that the sacrament is to be a positive experience, highlighting healing, rather than a punitive experience, dwelling on our sinfulness. Reconciliation rooms are to be set up so that the sacrament can be celebrated either in direct conversation with the priest or anonymously behind a screen. A Bible is often present in the reconciliation chapel, because reading from Scripture is part of the celebration, as suggested by the rite. A crucifix and candles may also be present to enhance the celebration and experience of prayer. These chapels are to be places of renewal that will offer refreshment for the penitent and revive them on their journey of faith so they may live the life that God offers them more fully. The architecture of the reconciliation chapel and all that is contained in it should support this experience of freedom from sin and reclaimed oneness with God and neighbor.

The Sacristy

Although given a somewhat lofty name, the sacristy is, in essence, a work area used to prepare for the celebration of the liturgy. The word "sacristy" comes from the Latin word *sacer,* which means "sacred." The sacristy is the place where sacred objects are stored, cleaned, and maintained. It is also the place where the ministers

get ready before the liturgy. In some churches, these two functions have resulted in two different sacristies: a working sacristy and a vesting sacristy. However, in most churches, both functions are housed in the same area.

Many objects that are used for the liturgy are cared for in the sacristy. The vestments that priests and deacons wear are stored there, as are the albs or cassocks and surplices worn by the altar servers. The sacred vessels, such as the chalices and patens, are stored, cleaned, and polished in the sacristy. It is also the place where other liturgical objects, such as the aspergillum, or sprinkling branch, and the thurible, or vessel of incense, are kept. This means that sacristies often include a safe to store such items as valuable gold vessels and a sink for general use.

Sacristies must also include a sacrarium. Again, the Latin word *sacer,* "sacred," is the root for this word. The sacrarium is a special sink that drains directly into the ground rather than draining into the sewer system. It is used for the washing of the sacred vessels after they have been purified. However, any Precious Blood that is left after Communion should be consumed. It is never to be poured into the sacrarium. The water used to purify the chalice and Communion cups is also to be consumed. Only the water used for the washing of the vessels after the purification may be poured into the sacrarium.

As mentioned, the sacristy is also the place where ministers ready themselves for the liturgy. This can, on occasion, turn the sacristy into a noisy and somewhat busy place right before the liturgy. Extraordinary ministers of holy Communion are confirming where to stand for the distribution of holy Communion. A lector is in a corner, reviewing the reading. Servers are putting on albs and may be jostling one another. The sacristan is trying to make sure everything and everyone is ready before liturgy begins. This makes it somewhat difficult to prepare mentally or spiritually for the celebration of the liturgy. This bustling activity was not always a part of the sacristy ambience. Priests used to quietly recite prayers while putting on their vestments to help them prepare for the celebration. In some sacristies, cards with these prayers are still present, or you can see them in the window above the priest's vesting table.

Although there are many details to attend to and many more people involved in preparing for the celebration of the liturgy, we might do well to reclaim some of the silence and prayerfulness in the sacristy as in years past. A prayer by all ministers before the liturgy begins does help. It will not only quiet everyone down, it will also focus all the ministers on the sacred tasks they are about to undertake.

Faithful Reflections

- ✠ *Do you remember praying in the church where you grew up as a child? Did you have a favorite chapel for praying or lighting a candle? Maybe you had a favorite saint you visited before or after Mass?*
- ✠ *Think about what drew you to that church and what compelled you to stay as you grew older. What images stand out that created a good experience for you? Was it the architecture? Was it the priest? The choir? The hospitality? What kind of church would you build if you had free reign and possibility? Draw or describe your ideal church or think about where you currently worship. What might you want to change?*
- ✠ *Does your church have a place for gathering? What is your experience of gathering as you arrive for worship? What creates that experience?*
- ✠ *Where is your baptismal font located? What is its shape and its size? Does it allow for a full experience of the sacrament of baptism? What does it express by its shape, size, and location?*
- ✠ *Is the place for reconciliation in your church inviting? How does this space affect your experience of the sacrament?*

CHAPTER FOUR

The Symbolic Meaning of Sacred Art

The Catholic Church, not unlike many other religions, has utilized the arts almost from its very inception to adorn its buildings, to enhance its liturgies, and to relay the narrative of the gospel. Working with sound and sight, in marble and wood, with brick and granite, artists have served the Church in its most essential tasks: to communicate and to celebrate the Good News. The outcome of this collaboration between the Catholic Church and innumerable artists, both known and unknown, can be found in the grand cathedrals, the welcoming churches, and the cozy chapels that are veritable treasure troves of religious art. And the relationship between the Church and the arts is confirmed by the many commissions that are realized even today throughout the world.

Thus, despite the occasional iconoclastic setback or artistic blunder, Christianity and the arts have successfully partnered in myriad ways for some 2,000 years. By virtue of its mere beauty, art has provided respite and hope in a world that often teeters on the precipice of chaos. By touching our minds, hearts, and souls, sacred art has offered unspoken insights into our shared human mysteries, such as life and death or love and hatred. And through its shapes, colors, textures, and composition, Christian art has supported our liturgical celebrations, illustrated our Christian narrative, and articulated our Christian values in ways that words cannot. Christian art affirms who we are as Christians and at the same time invites and challenges us to be better Christians— sometimes dramatically, but often in almost imperceptible ways.

SACRED ART THAT IS SPECIFICALLY CONCEIVED TO SERVE OUR LITURGIES IS KNOWN AS *LITURGICAL ART*, WHILE SACRED ART THAT SERVES THE DEVOTIONAL LIFE OF OUR CHURCH IS KNOWN AS *DEVOTIONAL ART*.

In a Catholic context, sacred art can be understood in a very broad and in a more defined way. Sacred art in general could be described as art that speaks to everything that is sacred and mysterious to humanity, such as the gifts of life and love and the challenges of human sin, suffering, and death. Narrowing it down a bit, sacred art that is specifically Christian tells the story of Christianity. Sacred art that is specifically conceived to serve our liturgies is known as *liturgical art*, while sacred art that serves the devotional life of our church is known as *devotional art*.

Popes and bishops alike have written extensively about the strong bond between the Catholic Church and the arts. *Sacrosanctum Concilium*, the 1963 Constitution on the Sacred Liturgy, which was the first document promulgated by the Second Vatican Council, affirms that "very rightly the fine arts are considered to rank among the noblest activities of human genius.... Holy Mother Church has therefore always been the friend of the fine arts and has ever sought their noble help."

Pope St. John Paul II, a poet and actor himself, touched often on art in his many writings and speeches. In his "Letter to Artists," he summarized the relationship between artists and the Church with three simple statements: "The Church needs artists. The Church needs musicians. The Church needs architects." On the tenth anniversary of the "Letter to Artists," the late Benedict XVI addressed a group of artists in the Sistine Chapel, saying, "You are the custodians of beauty: thanks to your talent, you have the opportunity to speak to the heart of humanity, to touch individual and collective sensibilities, to call forth dreams and hopes, to broaden the horizons of knowledge and of human engagement. Be grateful, then, for the gifts you have received and be fully conscious of your great responsibility to communicate beauty, to communicate in and through beauty! Through your art, you yourselves are to be heralds and witnesses of hope for humanity."

What Constitutes Sacred Art?

When French composer Maurice Ravel (1875–1937) publicly dedicated a newly composed string quartet to his teacher Gabriel Fauré (1845–1925), Fauré told him that this was very kind, but he would not accept the dedication because he hated the piece. He found it ugly, without meaning, and completely unintelligible. Publicly humiliated, Ravel doubted his musical talents and almost stopped composing. Thankfully, fellow composer Claude Debussy (1862–1918) encouraged him to continue his work as a composer. The piece in question, *String Quartet in F*, is a celebrated work in French string music, and Ravel is known and loved throughout the world.

The appreciation of art is often very subjective and depends mostly on the prevailing taste of a given society. Most of us are conditioned in terms of what we like by the leading vogues in broader society and the reigning tastes in the smaller communities we live in. Very few people venture beyond this comfort zone. Anything that is other than what we are used to is approached with suspicion, mistrust, or skepticism and is at best considered exotic or fantastical. And yet, one of the important tasks of artists is to take us out of that comfort zone and press us to face that which is other, sometimes uncomfortable, possibly unnerving.

Good artists possess the artistic skills to create something beautiful. Great artists, in addition, have the gift of vision. They see things and understand things we cannot see or understand, except when these artists allow us a peek into the world they see as depicted in their art. Sometimes, their vision is complex. Art can be unusual and maybe uncomfortable. If we don't immediately "like it," it doesn't mean that it is bad art. Some art takes more effort on our part to appreciate and understand.

The Catholic Church has always encouraged and welcomed the contributions of contemporary artists. That is why great medieval cathedrals of Europe house works by artists from each generation of believers who worshipped there over many centuries. For stylistic purists, the juxtaposition of old and new art is uncomfortable. However, as a Church, we are not interested in stylistic purity. Rather, we are interested in the ongoing expression of our faith in a style that not only intrigues and inspires us today but also can propel us into the future.

Recognizing the important contributions of contemporary artists to the artistic treasure trove of the Catholic Church, Pope Paul VI in 1973 established the Museum of Modern and Contemporary Religious Art as part of the Vatican Museums, thus assuring that the work of twentieth-century greats like Rouault and Matisse hangs mere meters away from work by such masters as Michelangelo and Raphael. More recently, Pope Francis' addition to the Vatican Museums is the Anima Mundi Museum, which houses indigenous art from Oceania, Africa, the Americas, and Asia. It was Pope Francis' express desire that this art be treated with the same awe and respect as the art of European masters.

Of course, in the same way that people have different tastes in most everything, they also have different tastes in sacred art, which often is relative to their spiritual sensitivities. Thus, while some Catholics might find fifteenth-century Madonnas too saccharine, others may be profoundly touched by them. That is why all sacred art ever made in the service of the Church needs to be treated with reverence and respect. The *General Instruction of the Roman Missal* states that the Church "is intent on preserving the works of art and artistic treasures handed down from past centuries." As an aside, it is not unusual to find a twenty-first-century abstract version of the Stations of the Cross in a Romanesque twelfth-century chapel next to a gothic fourteenth-century Madonna atop an eighteenth-century baroque altar. All are true expressions of the same faith but were created for a specific time and space. Again, this could be an absolute nightmare for the stylistic purist, yet to anyone who understands the artistic history of the Church and who relishes in the complementarity of these very different styles, their combined presence offers a wonderfully broad spectrum of the rich artistic traditions of the Catholic Church. In essence, they embody the rich diversity of generations of Catholics, each with their unique temperament, spirituality, and liturgical requirements, united in prayer within the same building.

Figurative Art, Abstract Art, and Non-Representational Art

Some of the works of art in our churches may be figurative, or representational, art; others may be abstract or non-representational art. Figurative art is always representational because it depicts a subject matter in a very representative way. A figurative representation of the crucifixion, e.g., clearly shows the crucifixion. And even though each artist offers their own interpretation of the crucifixion, it is not possible to mistake the subject matter of the figurative representation of the crucifixion.

Abstract and *non-representational* are

terms that are often used interchangeably as the opposite of figurative/representational art, yet there is a difference between abstract and non-representational art. An artist who works in abstraction presents an abstracted or even distorted image of specific subject matter. A good example is **Bernard Buffet's** *Veil of Veronica* (1961, Vatican Museums). Those of us who know the story immediately recognize it, but the figures are abstracted. This very abstraction underscores the tragedy of the encounter between Veronica and Jesus, who is carrying his cross on the way to his crucifixion. **Pablo Picasso,** who is not particularly known for religious art, took abstraction a step further in his 1930s painting of the crucifixion (1930, Musée Picasso, Paris). All the traditional elements of the crucifixion are there, but they are abstract and even distorted. It takes work on the part of the beholder to interpret the painting. Nevertheless, one still can tell that this is a painting of the crucifixion. Taking it another step further, in certain instances, one might not only need the help of art historians but also that of the artist to understand the painting. A good example is *Le Manteau de la Vierge Marie* ("*The Mantle of the Virgin*") by **Simon Hantai** (1962, Vatican Museums). Without the title, one would be hard-pressed to appreciate the painting to its fullest, although it is an an amazing work of art even without knowing what it represents.

Like all abstract art, these three examples show how the artist had a subject in mind while creating the art. Non-representational art, by contrast, does not start with specific subject matter carefully selected by the artist. And even if a non-representational artist had a subject in mind, you would never be able to tell from the resulting art. Non-representational art simply is what it is: splatters of paint or squares of color or even a blank canvas. A specific work of art may or may not express an emotion or feeling and may or may not evoke a corresponding emotional response in the beholder; in the end, it is up to the beholder to find meaning in it or not.

A figurative representation of a crucifixion leaves no doubt about the subject matter of the painting. Even those who are not familiar with the Christian narrative are able to deduce from the art that a man is being crucified. In the case of an abstract representation of the crucifixion, such as that by Pablo Picasso, it takes some work to figure it out, but it can be done. By contrast, even if a non-representational artist was thinking about the crucifixion when creating the art, the beholder would never be able to deduce that from simply viewing it.

As a result, figurative art is the most helpful to the mission of the Church, as its subject matter is clear and easily accessible. Yet, there is more to it. No matter how attractive a painting of the crucifixion might

be, if it does not draw us into the mystery of the cross and adore the One who died on it for our salvation, then the art has not done its work. What lies behind that which is shown is most important. What we see in figurative art is what the artist saw. Sometimes, we content ourselves with the vision of the artist as we deprive our religious imagination from entering into dialogue with that which is being represented.

By challenging the eyes and the mind of the beholder, abstract art tries to invite us beyond what we see in the painting. By deconstructing and abstracting familiar images, these artists point us in the direction of the true meaning of subject of the painting. Lucinda Naylor in her powerful *Stations of the Cross* (2000, Basilica of Minneapolis) takes it a step further and borders on the non-representational. Making use of the psychology of shapes and colors, Lucinda Naylor used simple strokes of black and purple to evoke dread in her abstract *Stations of the Cross*. She used red to evoke Jesus' suffering and bright white and yellow to evoke the joy of the resurrection.

If we are able to set aside our spontaneous likes and dislikes and open ourselves up to all forms of art, we will discover that there is a place for figurative art, abstract art, and even non-representational art in our liturgical celebrations and for our biblical narrations.

The Power of Art Experienced in the Most Unexpected Places

A local contemporary art museum once asked me to give a "Catholic" tour of an exhibit of works by South American artists titled *Ultra-Baroque*. The title intrigued me, as it referenced art of the Counter-Reformation, and giving a tour of this kind of art seemed an easy task for a Catholic art historian like me. It was with a certain level of panic that I perused the catalogue as I quickly realized that this exhibit had very little to do with art from the Counter-Reformation except to critique it. Baroque art had played a pivotal role in shaping the Church, culture, and even society in South America from the seventeenth century onward. The art in this exhibition was a reaction to the role of the Catholic Church and the use of baroque art as a powerful tool in the shaping of colonial societies.

When I visited the exhibit to prepare for my tour, I encountered a monumental work titled *Milagros*. It consisted of several very large versions of *milagros*, or "miracles," also known as *promesas*, or "promises." These are usually rather small images of failing body parts, often made of silver. They are brought to a sacred place, such as a Marian shrine, as a votive offering while praying for a miraculous cure. This custom was introduced to Central and South America by the Spanish and is still quite popular today.

Somewhat surprisingly, I was drawn to this work of art. While I was pondering its meaning, my mobile phone rang. My sister told me that my father was having emergency heart surgery. Suddenly, this contemporary work of art, which was not intended to inspire prayer, did just that. And this museum, which is dedicated to modern art often critical of organized religion, became a sacred place for me. Gazing at *Milagros,* I prayed for a miracle for my dad as I gazed upon the large *milagro* of a human heart.

To be clear, neither the setting nor the art was intended to be religious. However, the element of the sacred that is present in all good art, and which connects us with divine creative power, came to the surface to inspire me with hope and courage. And even though *Milagros* was created to mean one thing, it evoked a new meaning in me far beyond the intentions of the artist. That is the power of art.

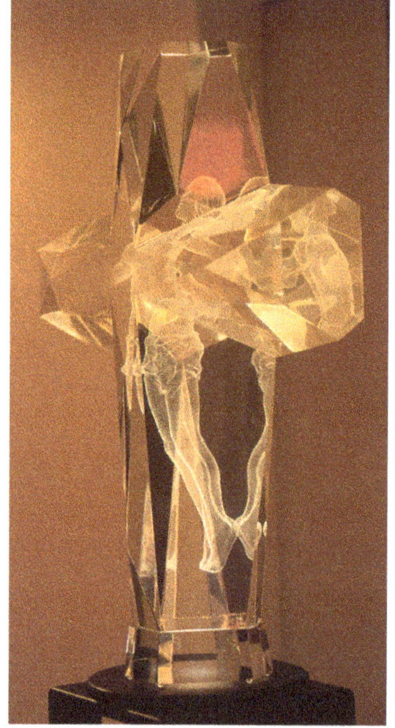

Because good art is born out of the artist's connectedness with divine creative power, it can communicate in ways that are neither intended by the artist nor foreseen by an art critic. Good art can communicate in very unexpected ways, beyond word or thought, revealing a deeper meaning. This kind of communication happens when a true encounter occurs between the art and the beholder. This kind of experience is not often the result of a lengthy thought process or an exercise to dissect the meaning of a specific work of art. It is more like falling in love. We don't reason ourselves into falling in love. It just happens, and, suddenly, we know. Art can work in a similar way. It does not explain; rather, it reveals and can do so in unexpected ways and in unexpected places. The art, the location, and the circumstances often come together, unplanned, when encounters of this kind take place.

However, not everyone "falls" in love. Some of us grow to love another person over time. This can also happen with art. For several months, I walked by a crucifix that had been created by the late Frederick Hart. It was displayed in the window of a local art gallery. I did not particularly like it because it was made of acrylic—and who likes acrylic sculptures? Despite that, I kept returning to the gallery to see it. It was as if the cross drew me back to itself, quietly but persistently. After weeks of peeking through the window, I entered the gallery to get a closer look. The owner saw me and smiled but left me alone. I went back to visit the cross several times, and one day the owner told me the story of the cross. When I got home, I could not get the cross out of my mind. The next day, I went back and purchased the cross for one of our chapels. The cross that I did not like at first has become one of my favorite pieces of art. In this case, I did not fall in love with the work of art; rather, I grew to love it. Good art, divinely inspired art, has a way of getting to you. Sometimes, as in the unexpected encounter with *Milagros,* it happens in the blink of an eye. Sometimes, as in the persistent yet unexpected revelation of the Frederick Hart cross, it takes time. In both instances, the impact was profound and lasting. In both instances, the art accomplished its sometimes-unexpected mission of giving hope, enriching faith, and ultimately drawing us closer to God. That is why good art, divinely inspired art, is uniquely equipped to spread the gospel and to serve the liturgy. Art has the power to move minds, hearts, and souls.

Sacred Art in Our Own Image

I grew up with an image of Mary and Jesus in my room. They both had rosy cheeks, blond hair, and blue eyes. This never struck me as odd until I realized that Mary and Jesus must have had dark skin, eyes, and hair because they were both Jewish and from the Middle East.

I have come to learn that most people tend to visualize Jesus, Mary, and the saints in a way that is typical for their own culture. This is known as the visual inculturation of religion. It means that the Christian narrative that is shared by all cultures is told in the visual image of the local culture. If you look at the medieval depiction of Mary in the Low Countries, including Belgium, you will see Mary depicted as a local aristocrat, sitting in a well-appointed room, wearing clothing typical for the time. She has Flemish almond eyes and pale skin. The Baby Jesus she carries looks Flemish, with his typical chubby cheeks. The same Mother and Child painted in the baroque period in Spain presents Mary as a Spanish baroque queen with darker skin and jet-black hair holding her Spanish child. A more recent sculpture of Mary and Child from Oceania, now housed in the Anima Mundi Museum in the Vatican, presents a very different image, reflective of the people of New Guinea.

All these depictions of Mary and Jesus are of course historically inaccurate. Yet, they are important because they testify to the fact that people of different cultures have identified with the Christian message. By depicting Mary and Jesus in their own image, each culture expresses and reinforces their belief that Jesus shared their humanity and died for their salvation. Inculturated images testify to the fact that different cultures made Christianity their own.

The aforementioned depictions of Mary and Jesus sprung from the artists' imaginations. Yet, Mary herself contributed to the diversity of her representation. The Blessed Mother knew that if the people she appeared to recognized themselves in her, they would be more welcoming of her. Thus, Our Lady of Guadalupe appeared as an Aztec princess, while Our Lady of La Vang in Vietnam appeared as a Huế woman. These and many other appearances have helped the faithful of different cultures understand more fully that she is not only the Jewish Mother of Jesus but also the mother of each one of us. Thus, while she remains the Mother of Jesus,

she has also come to be known in Mexico as Our Lady of Guadalupe, in Vietnam as Our Lady of La Vang, in Belgium as Our Lady of Banneux, and in Rwanda as Our Lady of Kibeho, to name but a few of her many apparitions.

Sacred Art and Evangelization

Throughout history, the Church has engaged the arts to assist with the spreading of the gospel, and still does so today. At first, art was used subtly to differentiate the tombs of Christians from non-Christian tombs. After Christianity became an accepted religion in the Roman Empire in 313, art was used to tell the Christian story and to illustrate the newly found importance of Christianity in society.

Art was a great evangelization tool during the Middles Ages, when most people were uneducated and illiterate. They learned about their faith by looking at the paintings, frescoes, stained-glass windows, and sculptures that depicted the stories of the Bible. These depictions were often described as the “Bible of the poor,” because they were the only way that the poor had access to Bible stories.

Baroque art and architecture were used during the Counter-Reformation to affirm the faith of the Church. Today, art continues to be an important ally in spreading the gospel message. Just think of Giotto’s frescoes in the Basilica of Saint Francis in Assisi, Leonardo da Vinci’s *Last Supper* in Milan, the *retablos* by named and unnamed *santeros* in the mission churches in New Mexico, and the amazing window of the Cathedral of Christ the Light in Oakland, California.

Much of our sacred art is directly inspired by the lives of Jesus, Mary, and the saints. Some art, however, evangelizes by highlighting the gospel values. A present-day artist who has committed his life to doing just that is Canadian artist Timothy Schmalz. He translates the often-challenging gospel message into powerful sculptures such as *The Homeless Jesus*, *Angels Unawares*, and *Let the Oppressed Go Free*.

During a walk in a park, Timothy Schmalz saw a man sleeping on a bench. He was immediately reminded of one specific line in Matthew 25:40: "[Jesus said,]'Whatever you did for one of these least brothers of mine, you did for me.'" That became his inspiration for ***The Homeless Jesus***. *The Homeless Jesus* depicts a man sleeping on a bench, wrapped in a blanket. His face is barely visible. Only his feet stick out of the blanket. The marks of the nails in his feet identify the person as Jesus.

Some people do not care for this sculpture because they prefer grand and glorious depictions of Jesus. Some even think that the sculpture is an insult to the risen Christ. Yet, it was Jesus himself who told us that he is every person who is hungry, thirsty, a stranger, naked, or imprisoned.

The Homeless Jesus is a quiet but strong visual sermon, a sculpted challenge, and a bronze invitation to authentic Christianity. It reminds us that we are to assist all those in need because in each one of them we ought to recognize Jesus.

Angels Unawares was commissioned in 2016 by Cardinal Czerny, who was tasked by Pope Francis to lead the Vatican's effort on behalf of migrants and refugees. The first cast of this sculpture is in Saint Peter's Square. This is the first and only sculpture added to the square, which was designed by Bernini and completed in 1667. The second cast is housed at Catholic University in Washington, DC.

Schmalz found his inspiration for *Angels Unawares* in the Letter to the Hebrews: "Do not neglect hospitality, for through it some have unknowingly entertained angels" (Hebrews 13:2).

Angels Unawares depicts 140 almost life-size people on a raft. They represent migrants from all times and all places. Sometimes, migrations happen by choice as people are looking for adventure, are driven by curiosity, or are responding to opportunity. Sometimes, migrations happen out of necessity as people flee war, persecution, hunger, natural disasters, and certain danger or even death. Sometimes, migrations happen by force as people are abducted from their homesteads and homelands and sent into endless misery or even sold into slavery.

The raft is obviously too small to hold all these people. It is intended to symbolize movement—the movement of migrants. It also draws attention to all the overcrowded boats and floating devices that are used in attempts to cross waterways on dangerous journeys in search of a better life.

Each figure on the raft represents an actual migrant. Schmalz used old photographs for migrants of the past, while current immigrants posed for him in his studio. Very poignantly, Schmalz represented the Holy Family—Jesus, Mary, and Joseph—amid this sea of migrants because they too were migrants, forced to flee their home out of fear that Herod might kill Jesus. An old man with a walking stick represents unknown ancient migrants and a young man who is seated at the back of the raft represents unknown current migrants who have left their homes in a quest for better lives for themselves and their families.

The wings of the unnamed angel mentioned

in Hebrews 13:2 hover over the center of the raft, warning us against neglecting or maltreating any of these migrants, for they might be "angels unawares."

Let the Oppressed Go Free, which was also commissioned by Cardinal Czerny, is inspired by Isaiah 58, in which God explains the true meaning of fasting, saying, "Is this not, rather, the fast that I choose: releasing those bound unjustly, untying the thongs of the yoke; Setting free the oppressed, breaking off every yoke? Is it not sharing your bread with the hungry, bringing the afflicted and the homeless into your house; Clothing the naked when you see them, and not turning your back on your own flesh?" (Isaiah 58: 6-7).

The one identifiable figure in the sculpture is St. Josephine Bakhita. As a young girl, she was abducted from her village in Sudan and sold into slavery at the end of the nineteenth century. After having been mistreated by different slave owners, she ended up in the household of an Italian diplomat who took her to Italy. Because Italy did not recognize slavery, St. Josephine became a free woman.

She converted to Christianity and became a Canossian sister. She was the cook and doorkeeper at the Canossian Convent in Schio, Italy, for forty-two years. She is said to have been gentle and charismatic, and the people in Schio saw her as their protector, especially during World War II. After her canonization in 2000, she became the patroness of people who are experiencing modern-day enslavement.

While describing his inspiration for the sculpture, Schmalz referenced the famous folktale of the Pied Piper of Hamelin. He explained that when the piper wasn't paid for removing the rats, he played another tune, and the ground opened up, sucking the town's children into

the underground. Similarly, human trafficking forces children and adults underground. The sculpture shows victims of human trafficking being finally released from that underground by St. Josephine Bakhita. This sculpture draws our attention to the often hidden evil of human trafficking and calls on us to do all we can to set the oppressed free.

Sacred Art and Celebration

In addition to spreading the gospel, architecture, art, and music greatly enhance the celebration of the liturgy and support the devotional life of the Church. It is impossible to imagine Catholic liturgy and devotions without the arts. The primary reason for the construction of cathedrals, churches, and chapels is to house our liturgy and devotions. Their adornment with art is intended to enhance the spiritual experience of our celebrations. Liturgical and devotional furnishings, objects, and vesture are designed and constructed to specifically serve them. Liturgical and devotional music plays a crucial role in supporting ritual acts and movements, thereby aiding the community in prayer.

Defining what this kind of art looks or sounds like is somewhat difficult. In more general terms, if the earthly celebration of liturgy is indeed a foreshadowing of the heavenly liturgy, then the arts need to warrant that. And if our liturgy and devotions are a portal to the divine and the locus for epiphanies to happen, then the liturgical arts need to support that. As a result, some theologians and artists require devotional art, especially liturgical art, to be characterized by an "aesthetic of heaven."

Requiring an aesthetic of heaven is a worthy expectation, because liturgical art indeed needs to offer a glimpse of heaven and open a

window into heaven. The stylistic implications of this aesthetic are less clear, as the effectiveness of sacred art is dependent not only upon the art itself but also upon the spiritual sensitivity and sensibilities of each place, time, and individual that receive the art. Some people's aesthetic of heaven is most fully and even exclusively embodied by classical architectural forms and by the use of costly materials worthy of the mystery they bespeak and celebrate. Others hold an opposite opinion and believe that the sacredness of art and architecture can neither be held hostage by style nor by material. They believe that those who worship in the Matisse Chapel in Provence, in adobe churches in New Mexico, or in churches inspired by African architectural principles and materials in Kenya may very well experience a desire for the heavenly Jerusalem that is as great as, if not greater than, that of those who worship in the most perfect examples of classical architecture accentuated by marble, granite, gold leaf, and silk.

Yet, no matter our opinion on appropriateness of style, if we were to strip our sacred spaces and liturgical celebrations of all artistic endeavors, there would be scarcely anything left. Architecture, art, poetry, and music are essential to the celebration of our liturgy and our devotions.

Sacred Art and Devotions

Art has not only been used to support and enhance the communal celebration of the liturgy, but many private and public religious devotions also center on works of art. The Stations of the Cross are a perfect example of art that serves our devotions. This specific devotion, which is a spiritual journey through the last days of Jesus' life, is rooted in a deep human need to see, touch, and experience places of personal, historic, or religious importance that were related to Jesus.

Sometimes, people will travel thousands of miles to remember and be present in a particular place or visit an object that is full of meaning. Catholic football fans often travel across the country to visit the football stadium at Notre Dame and touch the statue of famed football coach Knute Rockne. Each year, millions of Catholics go to Rome to visit the tombs of the early martyrs and to pray with the pope. Muslims, Jews, and Christians alike visit Jerusalem, a place that is held holy by all three of these major religions.

The desire to visit places of importance for Christians, such as Jerusalem, is not new. As soon as Emperor Constantine legalized Christianity, the number of pilgrims to Jerusalem increased rapidly. Saint Helena, Constantine's mother, became one of the most influential pilgrims. Not only did she find many important relics, such as the crown of thorns and the True Cross, she also had churches built over the most important sacred sites. And the Via Dolorosa, or the Way of Sorrow, was developed in Jerusalem, tracing the journey of Jesus from his condemnation to his burial.

Ever since, Christians have visited these sites. And when they returned to their homelands, they brought back compelling stories and vivid descriptions of their experiences. These captivating stories resulted in a growing emphasis on the salvific passion of Jesus. This devotion that followed the events of Jesus on his journey from his trial to his tomb developed quickly and was promoted by the Franciscan friars through their preaching. This gave rise to the construction of shrines dedicated to Jesus' passion, often copying the shrines in Jerusalem.

In some churches, a series of chapels (or "stations") were built, reminiscent of the many sacred sites in Jerusalem. This eventually resulted in Stations of the Cross in many churches, which, in essence, is a virtual visit to the sacred sites in Jerusalem that mark Jesus' passion and death. Those who cannot make the journey to the Holy Land can participate in a "mini pilgrimage" in a church close to home.

Stations of the Cross varied from place to place, and the number of stations ranged from seven to thirty. The fourteen Stations of the Cross we know today were codified by Pope Clement XII in 1731 and are still the most popular, yet others exist as well.

During the annual celebration of the Stations of the Cross in the Coliseum in Rome on Good Friday, 1991, Pope St. John Paul II introduced a new version of Stations of the Cross. This version differs in two ways from the traditional devotion. First, the content of each one of these stations is biblically based. Thus, though spiritually meaningful, such stations as "Jesus meets Veronica" or "Jesus falls three times," which have no direct biblical reference, were replaced. By ensuring the biblical foundation of each one of the stations, the late Pope intended to make the stations accessible to all Christians. Second, Pope St. John Paul II added a fifteenth station representing the resurrection. His reasoning was that without the resurrection, the passion and death of Jesus make absolutely no sense.

Different churches display their stations in different ways. The most common presentation is for the images of the stations to be mounted on the outer perimeter walls of the church. This placement allows people to walk from one station to the next and experience the movement of a pilgrimage. Some churches have located their stations outside, on church grounds. This allows for even more time and space to journey from one station to the next. The depictions of the stations can be figurative or abstract, elaborate or minimal, bronze cast or painted on wood, made in mosaics or sculpted in stone, but, for the Stations of the Cross to be celebrated, depictions are needed.

Other devotions also rely heavily on the arts. Statues are often the focal point of shrines dedicated to Jesus, Mary, and the saints. We surround our saints with candles. We dress them in regal garb or give them elaborate crowns. We carry them on our shoulders and process them through our cities. We touch their feet, their hands, or their heads. We decorate them with flowers and wreaths. None of these important aspects of our devotional life could happen without the efforts of artists in providing depictions of Jesus, Mary, and the saints. These depictions are constant reminders of what the saints have done for us and continue to do. They invite us to pray with them for the needs of the world. And they encourage us to imitate them in our own lives so that we may become more like them.

Faithful Reflections

We receive information in many ways as we grow from a small child to an adult person. What are your first memories of learning about Jesus and the Gospel stories? Was it through a story, a book, a painting, or a stained-glass window in church?

For some 2,000 years, the Church has engaged the arts to tell the story of our faith, to enhance our liturgical celebrations, and to promote our devotions. Imagine how you might depict the gospel. What are ways to tell a story of faith without words? Think about what colors or shapes you associate with different experiences of prayer: silence, praise, lamentation, intercession. Now, create a prayer without words.

- ✠ *How is art used to enhance the liturgies at your church? What would you like to see?*
- ✠ *What kinds of devotions are encouraged by the works of art in your church? How do these works of art help you pray?*
- ✠ *How can you incorporate art in your home to support your life of faith and prayer? What is a favorite religious image that might help you create a prayer?*

CHAPTER FIVE

The Symbolic Meaning of Liturgical Furnishings

Many of us enhance the aesthetics of our home by painting the walls in pleasing colors, adorning them with art, and strategically placing furniture throughout the house. Each room in the house is assigned a specific function that, for very practical reasons, requires corresponding furnishings. Because we sleep in our bedroom, that is where we place the bed. To accommodate communal dining in the kitchen or dining room, we make sure it contains a table and chairs. The primary function of a living room is conversation and relaxation, which calls for comfortable chairs and a sofa.

Similarly, our churches are appointed with furnishings that serve the celebration of the different sacraments that take place there. Each sacrament requires its own furnishings. Baptisms happen in a baptismal font, and the Eucharist is celebrated at an altar. Unlike the furnishings in our home, which are merely practical, liturgical furnishings are both practical and symbolic. A baptismal font is more than just a receptacle of water, and an altar is much more than just a table at which the Eucharist is celebrated. Because of this, all liturgical furnishings must be of high aesthetic quality and should comply with the norms established by the Church.

UNLIKE THE FURNISHINGS IN OUR HOME, WHICH ARE MERELY PRACTICAL, LITURGICAL FURNISHINGS ARE BOTH PRACTICAL AND SYMBOLIC.

The Altar Table

On Ash Wednesday, in an unnamed parish, the choir sings the evening Mass, shares a simple soup supper, and has a meditative rehearsal in the chapel. Unlike the main church, the chapel is rather contemporary and is set up in choir style, with the altar in the center and chairs on either side. That year, Easter was early, and it was cold and snowy on Ash Wednesday. Choir members had been lugging their heavy coats around all evening. They now plopped them on the chapel chairs because no coat rack was available. Regrettably, some choir members had placed their coats on the altar. The pastor was to begin the rehearsal with a Lenten meditation. As they were awaiting the pastor's arrival, choir members were happily chatting with one another. When the pastor arrived, he saw the coats on the altar. Without saying a word, he marched up to the altar and, in one fell swoop, swiped it clean of all the coats. After a communal gasp, there was instantaneous silence. With this dramatic gesture, the pastor had made it abundantly clear that the altar is not just a piece of furniture. The altar, once consecrated, is a symbol of Christ, both during and outside the celebration of the Eucharist. That is exactly the lecture that the choir members were embarrassed to receive. The altar has not been used as a coat rack again.

Many religions have made ritual use of altars. Some built them on the tops of soaring mountain peaks, near the edges of dormant volcanoes, or on the banks of rushing rivers. Altars were found in temples, cathedrals, churches, and chapels. In most instances, they were built to perform some kind of offering or sacrifice on. This offering may have consisted of pouring wine or oil on the altar, as in Leviticus 23. Or the altar may have served as a place for burnt offerings of wheat and barley, such as in the second chapter of Leviticus. It may have been where an animal was sacrificed, such as in the first chapter of Leviticus. In some religions,

altars were even used for human sacrifice. A Christian altar table stands out because it is not only the place where the sacrifice of the Mass is celebrated but also the principal place of gathering for the followers of Jesus.

Throughout Christianity's history of more than 2,000 years, Christian altars have evolved from a low table where Christ and the disciples reclined at the time of the Last Supper, to a movable table in early basilicas, to an ornate construction fixed to the back wall of the church where the priest celebrated Mass with his back to the people and sometimes even hidden from sight by ceremonial curtains. Since the Second Vatican Council, the altar is now placed closer to the assembly so that the faithful can truly gather around the altar at which the Mass is celebrated.

Christian altars are made of all sorts of materials. There are massive stone altars that emphasize the sacrificial character of the Eucharist. There are simple wooden altars that underscore the altar as a table around which Christians gather. Some altars incorporate wood and stone to highlight both sacrifice and gathering. Although the Church does not offer specifics for the design of an altar, the *General Instruction of the Roman Missal* holds that "the altar, on which is effected the sacrifice of the Cross made present under sacramental signs, is also the table of the Lord to which the people of God is convoked to participate in the Mass, and it is also the center of the thanksgiving that is accomplished through the Eucharist" (*GIRM* 296).

Unlike other liturgical furnishings, the altar is considered a symbol of Christ because the sacrifice of the Mass is celebrated on it. The ritual for the *Dedication of a Church and an Altar (DCA)* states that "the Church's writers have seen in the altar a sign of Christ himself. This is the basis for the saying: 'the altar is Christ'" (*DCA* 4).

Because of their sacred character, altars are "vested" with beautiful altar linens. Nothing should be placed on the altar except what is needed for the celebration of the Eucharist. The altar is reverenced by all ministers with a bow and by ordained ministers with a kiss at

the beginning and end of the liturgy. And the altar is honored with incense during the opening procession and at the time of the offertory.

The Ambo

The ambo is a place from where the word of God is proclaimed. Unlike the altar, which is truly a symbol of Christ, the ambo is not; rather, the *Gospel Book* from which the word of God is proclaimed is a symbol of Christ and thus receives the respect it is due. That is why the *Gospel Book* is incensed, but the ambo is not, before the proclamation of the gospel.

Nevertheless, because the word of God is proclaimed from the ambo, it is considered a place of importance. Its prominence and design should enable the assembly to hear and see the lector while the word of God is being proclaimed. Eye contact is very important, as it allows the assembly to listen better and receive the word more fully.

The location, design, and material of the ambo should call attention to the importance of the word of God during the liturgy and should allow it to function as a place of efficacious proclamation. The ambo should be accessible by all lectors, regardless of their physical abilities.

The Font

Although early Christians required only running water for the celebration of the sacrament of baptism, the container for baptismal water gained importance over the course of the centuries. What began as a simple statement, such as "Look, there is water. What is to prevent my being baptized?" (Acts 8:36) uttered by the eunuch in response to the Apostle Phillip, has evolved to baptismal fonts that are architecturally complex and symbolically rich.

While rivers were the preferred places for early Christian baptisms, baptisms were soon moved inside. At first, Roman baths were used. Then, buildings were designed specifically to celebrate the sacrament of baptism; these are known as *baptisteries*.

Because water is the primary symbol for baptism, early fonts were large and deep to allow for immersion, which was how most Christians were baptized. However, due to the decrease of adult baptism in favor of infant baptism, the fonts grew smaller and were no longer built into the ground. Rather, they were placed on pedestals to accommodate the baptism of infants more easily. As the mode of baptizing changed from immersion to affusion, or the pouring of water, less water was needed. Thus, the basins of the fonts became smaller as well. In addition, to prevent baptismal water from

being stolen for use in witchcraft, locked covers were placed on top of fonts, and the fonts themselves were placed behind locked doors. The primary baptismal symbol of water was henceforth relegated to a small basin with a locked and behind a gate.

Since the Second Vatican Council's reinstitution of the Order of Christian Initiation of Adults (OCIA) encouraged a return to immersion as the norm for baptism, a greater emphasis has again been placed on water, rather than on its container, as the symbol for baptism. To accommodate immersion, more water is needed, which necessitates larger and more accessible fonts. As a result, the baptismal font in many contemporary churches has a larger basin. The font is often very visible and located in a prominent place in the church, such as near the entrance of the church or even in the gathering space to emphasize that baptism is the first sacrament we receive and the sacrament by which we enter the Church. Another location is the center of the church, allowing the community to be present to the sacrament of baptism and symbolizing that, through baptism, the neophyte is birthed into the Church. A third possible location is in the sanctuary, again allowing the assembly to be present to the sacrament and connecting the sacrament of baptism to the sacrament of the Eucharist. In some instances, the location of the font is highlighted by dedicated lights or even by some kind of canopy that is suspended above the font.

The shape of the font provides additional context for understanding the sacrament. Some fonts are octagonal, or eight-sided, to remind us of the eighth day, the day of the resurrection. These fonts symbolize how the neophytes, or newly baptized, share in the resurrection of Christ through their baptism. Other fonts are hexagonal, or six-sided, pointing to the sixth day, or Friday, when we commemorate the death of Jesus. These fonts, like cruciform fonts and tomb-like fonts, symbolize that in order to rise with Christ, we need to die with him in the waters of baptism. There are also round fonts, offering a reference to the font as the womb through which baptized neophytes are born into the Church.

If possible, a font should be placed on a west-to-east axis, which allows those to be baptized to enter the font from the west and rise from the baptismal waters facing east—facing the direction from where Christ will return at the end of time.

In addition to its shape, the font's symbolic meaning may be highlighted by the addition of some carefully chosen decorative elements, such as Jonah exiting the whale (See Jonah 2.), after the example of ancient baptismal fonts. Care should be taken not to obscure the water—the true symbol of baptism—with secondary symbols. No matter the shape or location of the font, it is, in all cases, the primary symbol of the water it holds that gives the font its meaning as the place where new Christians are made.

The Celebrant's Chair: Bishop, Priest, and Deacon

The role of the celebrant is to lead the community in prayer. His place in the assembly should therefore support that purpose. The celebrant's chair must be located in such a way that he can easily lead the service. Its design should befit the leader of the community. At the same time, the chair of the celebrant is not to be confused with a throne because the priest is the servant leader of the community, and his seat should reflect that humility.

The celebrant's chair is to be used only by the celebrating priest. When a lay leader is celebrating in the absence of a priest, he or she may not use this chair. Lay leaders are to sit with the assembly and come forward to face the assembly at appointed times during the liturgy when they lead the community in prayer. This practice emphasizes that lay leaders are called forth from the assembly, and the empty chair symbolizes the absence of an ordained minister. A deacon who leads a Sunday Celebration in the Absence of a Priest, though ordained, also should not sit in the celebrant's chair. He should sit in the deacon's chair, leaving the celebrant's chair unoccupied.

In his own cathedral, a bishop has a special chair reserved for him. The word "cathedral" is derived from the Latin word *cathedra,* which means "chair." This chair symbolizes the bishop's office. The cathedral is therefore the church with the bishop's chair. Because of this, the period when a diocese is without a bishop is known as *sede vacante,* or "empty

chair," meaning that there is no one to occupy the cathedra.

The custom of using a cathedra goes back to Roman times, when leaders of the empire pronounced judgments and new rulings while seated in chairs that symbolized their offices. Pilate, for instance, sat in the judgment seat when condemning Jesus to death. (See John 19: 13–16.) Because the office of the bishop and the customs surrounding it were more clearly defined during Roman times, some Roman customs, such as the use of a cathedra, were adopted by the Church, and the cathedra came to symbolize the office of the bishop.

Traditionally, the bishop's chair is designed to be a bit more substantial and more ornate than the celebrant's chair. It is often personalized for each successive bishop by adding his personal coat of arms.

Tabernacle

According to the Hebrew Scriptures, the tabernacle was a portable tent in which Moses was instructed by God to house the Ark of the Covenant. The word "tabernacle" comes from the Latin *tabernaculum*, which means "tent." The Hebrew term used for the tabernacle implies that it is a place to dwell, to rest, to live. It is the place that houses the presence of God on earth.

A tabernacle in the Catholic tradition has its roots in the Jewish tradition, as it houses God's presence on earth par excellence: the Body of Christ. *GIRM* stipulates that "in accordance with the structure of each church and legiti-

mate local customs, the Most Blessed Sacrament should be reserved in a tabernacle in a part of the church that is truly noble, prominent, readily visible, beautifully decorated, and suitable for prayer.... The one tabernacle should be immovable, be made of solid and inviolable material that is not transparent, and be locked in such a way that the danger of profanation is prevented to the greatest extent possible." The document goes on to state that "it is more in keeping with the meaning of the sign that the tabernacle in which the Most Holy Eucharist is reserved not be on an altar on which Mass is celebrated" (*GIRM* 314–315).

A lamp that is kept alight should be placed near the tabernacle "to indicate and honor the presence of Christ" (*GIRM* 316).

Faithful Reflections

What preparations do you make when you are planning a birthday dinner or a more formal meal for guests who are invited to your home? Often, we think through where people will sit, what kind of dishes and glassware we will use, and if we have enough chairs for everyone who will attend. While these preparations can become an event in and of themselves, there is usually a greater meaning for the gathering that exceeds the practical yet purposeful needs at hand. Sometimes, there is even a special plate for the main course or a specific chair for the birthday girl or boy.

Liturgical furnishings serve a similar, though elevated, double role. First, liturgical furnishings are very practical, as they serve a specific liturgical purpose. The celebrant needs a place to sit. The bread and wine need to be placed on a table. Second, some of the furnishings also have a deeply symbolic meaning. The altar is the place of sacrifice and the table for the body of Christ to gather. The ambo is the place of proclamation of the Word of God. The celebrant's chair is the place where the celebrant presides over the liturgy. Now, think about the liturgical furnishings in your church.

- ✠ *What do your church's altar and ambo look like? What shape do they share? What materials are they made of?*
- ✠ *How large is your church's font? Can you see and touch the water? Does it allow for immersion? What can you learn about baptism by looking at your font?*
- ✠ *Where is the celebrant's chair located? How does it support the role of a servant leader of the community?*

CHAPTER SIX

The Symbolic Meaning of Liturgical Objects

Every year, a group of parishioners at the Basilica of Saint Mary in Minneapolis prepare an Easter fire that will be blessed during the Great Easter Vigil later that day, on Holy Saturday. They place a twelve-foot cauldron in the center of the plaza in front of the basilica, and they fill it with wood. After the sun has set, they light the fire while parishioners start to gather around. The first to arrive are the elect who will be initiated into the Church that night. They stand closest to the fire with eager excitement. Slowly, the entire area fills up with people who are looking forward to celebrating the resurrection of the Lord.

Every year, the church requests a fire permit from the city and advises the fire department that an Easter fire will be lit, because inevitably someone will call and tell them that the Basilica is on fire. A highway runs nearby, and traffic slows as people crane their necks to get a glimpse of what's going on. The power of the pre-symbolic human experience of fire and the power of liturgical symbols, such as the Easter fire, are on full display that night.

THERE ARE MANY LITURGICAL SYMBOLS USED FOR THE CELEBRATION OF OUR SACRAMENTS. WE MIGHT RECOGNIZE THEM BY SIGHT, BUT WE MIGHT NOT KNOW THEIR NAMES, WHAT THEY ARE USED FOR, WHERE THEY ARE FROM, OR WHAT THEY MEAN.

Liturgical practice necessitates and is enriched by the utilization of various liturgical items. These range from obviously liturgical objects, such as a crucifix and a chalice, to more obscure ones, such as the Easter fire. Some of them were specifically designed for Catholic worship, while others were borrowed from pre-Christian societies. Together, they allow for a meaningful celebration of the Christian mysteries.

Cross and Crucifix

The most recognizable symbols of Christianity today are undoubtedly the cross and crucifix. The difference between the two is that the crucifix is a cross with a representation of the crucified Jesus, or *corpus*, nailed to the cross. Catholics seem to favor the crucifix, while many other Christian denominations prefer the cross.

Though both the cross and crucifix are now commonplace, this has not always been the case. Early Christians used other symbols, such as a fish or an anchor, to identify themselves. This is not surprising because, according to Jewish belief, the Messiah will never die. To the Jewish followers of Jesus, the fact that he died must have been quite an enigma, especially before they experienced the resurrection. If Jesus was indeed the Messiah, which they believed, how could he have died? As a result, his death was at first underemphasized in favor of his resurrection. The cross was the sign of ultimate humiliation in the Roman world, and, as such, it took some time for Christians to embrace this instrument of torture that became our pathway to salvation.

The first known depiction of a crucifix dates to the second century. It is a type of early Roman graffiti with a very sarcastic rendition of the crucifixion. It depicts a human with the head of a donkey nailed to the cross. A Greek inscription reads "Alexamenos worships his God." Clearly, the person who created this image intended to ridicule Alexamenos and his religion.

Christians tentatively started to use a cross, at first surrounded by a victory wreath, emphasizing Jesus' victory over death. It was not until the beginning of the fifth century that Christians began to display crucifixes. In these early versions, Jesus stands with both feet nailed separately to the cross. His eyes are open and there is no sign of suffering. He is clearly in control of this situation. A great example is a small panel in the fifth-century wooden doors of Santa Sabina in Rome.

Gradually, Christians became more comfortable with Jesus' suffering on the cross. By the tenth century, depictions showed a slightly sagging body and signs of human suffering. Also, Jesus was no longer standing on the cross, as one nail was pounded through both feet, which were placed on top of one another. By the fourteenth and fifteenth centuries, the body of Jesus began to be depicted with the many wounds he suffered from being repeatedly whipped.

The depiction of the suffering Jesus was very popular during times of war, famine, and suffering. It allowed the people to identify with the suffering of Jesus and to comprehend on a deeply personal level how Jesus had suffered for them. A famous example is the early sixteenth-century altarpiece by **Matthias Grünewald**. This painting was commissioned for the hospital chapel of Saint Anthony's Monastery in Isenheim, France. Many patients in the hospital were treated for ergotism, commonly known as "St. Anthony's fire," which caused hallucinations and skin infections. Grünewald depicted Jesus on the cross in the image of those suffering from ergotism. When they attended Mass, they would gaze upon Jesus on the cross and were able to connect his suffering with their suffering.

Today, we see crucifixes that emphasize the suffering of Jesus as well as those that point to the resurrection. Some crucifixes even bear the risen Christ.

A particular type of crucifix is the processional cross. It is used at the beginning of most liturgical processions, specifically during and at the end of Mass. By following behind the cross in procession, we are visually reminded that we are followers of Christ. The use of a processional cross pre-dates the placement of a crucifix near or on the altar. The earliest version of an altar cross was actually the crucifix

on the processional cross, which was detached from its pole at the end of the procession.

A great example of a processional cross is a typical Orthodox icon cross, with its complex symbology and theology. Jesus is depicted at the time of his death. And though he had clearly suffered, the Orthodox tradition depicts Jesus with respect and dignity. He holds the palms of his hands upward, as if in a divine embrace. Two nails are used for Jesus' feet, allowing him to stand on the cross. He also has the wound of the spear that was used by the Roman soldier Longinus to pierce his side. It is believed that Longinus is the one who exclaimed, "Truly, this was the Son of God!" (Matthew 27:54).

Rather than wearing the crown of thorns, Jesus wears the cruciform halo, indicating that even in death, Jesus is truly God. This is also affirmed by the three Greek letters **Ο Ω Ν** (omicron, omega, and nu), meaning **ὁ ὤν** or "He Who Is." This is a reference to the revelation of the name of God to Moses in the burning bush affirming that Jesus, even in death, is God.

The wall beneath the cross is the symbol for the city, Jerusalem, where Jesus was crucified "outside the walls." It is also a reference to the heavenly Jerusalem, where all of us are welcome by virtue of Jesus' life, death, and resurrection.

Under the cross, you can see a skull in a cave. Often, people think this is a reference to Golgotha, the "place of the skull." This is true, but there is more to it. According to early Fathers of the Church, such as Origen, St. John Chrysostom, and St. Jerome, Jesus was crucified on the tomb of Adam. Epiphanius of Salamis (c. 315–403) wrote that "Adam later came and died in this place, I mean Jerusalem, and was buried there, on the site of Golgotha." Whether true or not, the notion of Jesus being crucified on the tomb of Adam symbolizes the theological truth that through Adam, sin and death were brought into the world. Through the life, death, and resurrection of the new Adam, Jesus, forgiveness and life was brought back into the world.

To Jesus' right, you can see Mary, his mother; to his left, you can see John the beloved. On either side of Mary and John are depictions of the sun and moon, clouds, and stars. According to Matthew, Mark, and Luke the sun and moon darkened at the time of the crucifixion, as the death of Jesus was a cosmic event. Above Jesus' head is a board inscribed with the letters INRI: the first letters of the Latin *Iesus Nazarenus Rex Iudeaorum*, which means "Jesus of Nazareth, King of the Jews." Above that, two angels are holding the sponge on a reed used to give Jesus vinegar to drink, the lance used to pierce his side, and the crown of thorns.

On the very top is the Holy Napkin. There are two traditions behind this image. According to the Western tradition, Veronica walked up to Jesus as he was carrying his cross and soothed his face with a cloth. The image of Jesus' face appeared on the cloth. The name "Veronica" comes from the Greek *vera icon,* meaning "true image." According to the Orthodox tradition, the King of Edessa sent word to Jesus that he was sick, asking Jesus to come and heal him.

Jesus sent one of the disciples with a piece of cloth on which the face of Jesus appeared, and the king was healed. This cloth is known as the Mandylion of Edessa, *mandylion* being the Greek word for "small cloth or towel."

Easter Candle or Paschal Candle

Who does not like to light candles? It is a delight to watch young parents bring their children to light votive candles. They carefully light a candle and place it in its holder, then stare at it for such a long time that I wonder what they are thinking. Maybe they are not thinking at all and are allowing the symbol of the light to be their visual prayer.

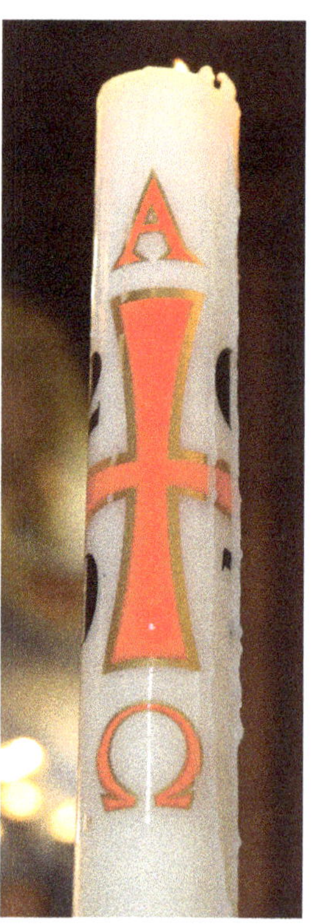

Light plays an important role in many religions. It often symbolizes the victory of good, represented by light, over evil, symbolized by darkness. Light also adds ambiance or sets the mood of a gathering. The more important the dinner party, the taller the candelabras and the greater the number of candles we display. This also holds true for the use of candles at liturgy. At the most important of all liturgies, the celebration of the Easter Vigil, we use the most beautiful and the tallest candle of them all—the Easter candle.

Every year, at the beginning of the Easter Vigil on Holy Saturday, a new Easter candle, also known as the paschal candle or the Christ candle, is lit from the Easter fire and then blessed. The blessing consists of two prayers and a number of accompanying liturgical actions. The first prayer reads as follows:

Christ, yesterday and today,
the Beginning and the End
the Alpha and the Omega,
all time belongs to him and all the ages;
to him be glory and power
through every age and for ever.
Amen.

While saying this prayer, the priest first carves a cross into the candle, followed by the letters A and Ω and the number of the year of salvation. Today, most Easter candles have the cross, the A and Ω, and the year pre-drawn so that the priest just signs them on the candle.

Then, the priest says the second prayer:

By his holy and glorious wounds
may Christ our Lord guard us and keep us.
Amen.

During this prayer, the priest inserts five grains of incense, often encased in wax-covered nails, into the candle. These grains of incense and nails represent the five wounds Christ suffered in his hands, feet, and side.

Once the Easter candle is blessed, it is lit from the Easter fire and raised high while the priest sings, "The light of Christ." The people then respond, "Thanks be to God," and everyone lights their own candle from the Easter candle. This symbolizes that all the baptized share in the light of Christ and are called to be light to the world. The candle is then placed near the ambo, where it remains for the entire

Easter season. As the liturgy continues, the paschal candle will be plunged three times into the baptismal water during the blessing of the water. This dunking symbolizes that Christ is fertilizing the baptismal womb from where new Christians will be born. During the Easter season, the paschal candle is honored with incense at the beginning of the liturgy and during the preparation of the altar and gifts, just like the crucifix in the sanctuary.

Outside of the Easter season, the Easter candle resides near the baptismal font. Baptismal candles are lit from the Easter candle during the celebration of baptisms throughout the entire liturgical year to symbolize that the newly baptized share in the resurrection of Christ. At funerals, the Easter candle is placed next to the coffin or the urn to symbolize Christ's resurrection and our participation in it through our baptism.

Liturgical Books: *Gospel Book*, *Lectionary*, and *Missal*

Of the many books we use for the celebration of the liturgy, the *Gospel Book* is the most important because it contains the word of God as revealed to the four evangelists: Matthew, Mark, Luke, and John. The designation *evangelist* comes from the Greek, meaning "bringer of good news." Because it contains the Good News of Jesus Christ, the *Gospel Book* is one of the principal liturgical symbols of Christ.

Due to its great significance, the *Gospel Book* is carried by the deacon or by the lector in the entrance procession of the liturgy. It is then carefully placed on the altar. During the Liturgy of the Word, the one who is proclaiming the gospel retrieves the *Gospel Book* from the altar. Flanked by candles and accompanied by incense, he processes the *Gospel Book* from the altar to the ambo while everyone sings the gospel acclamation. Upon arrival at the ambo, the *Gospel Book* is honored with incense and solemnly proclaimed by the deacon or priest. After the proclamation, the *Gospel Book* is honored with a kiss. When the bishop is present, the *Gospel Book* may be brought to him to kiss, and he may bless the people with the *Gospel Book*. Then, the *Gospel Book* is set in a place of honor for the remainder of the liturgy.

The *Gospel Book* should be treated with respect at all times because it is a symbol of Christ. The book itself should be one of substance to indicate the importance of the word

of God in our Church and in the liturgy. For centuries, the *Gospel Book* has been beautifully designed and decorated, sometimes with a metal or a leather cover to both protect it and enhance its appearance.

The *Gospel Book* itself or its cover often are elaborately decorated and include imagery, such as a symbolic representation of the four evangelists. This image is known as the Tetramorph (see pages 137–138). Sometimes, the book cover depicts Christ by himself or Christ surrounded by the four evangelists.

In most churches, the *Gospel Book* is kept in the sacristy. Some churches have a special area where the *Gospel Book* is enshrined outside of the liturgy. Such placement emphasizes the importance of this book. Other churches place the *Gospel Book*, opened to the gospel of the day, on a ledge on the front side of the ambo. Wherever it is kept, the *Gospel Book* must be stored with great care in a respectful way, as it remains a symbol of Christ both during and outside of the celebration of the liturgy.

The *Lectionary* is used during Mass. This book contains all the liturgical readings for every day of the liturgical year. On Sunday, the *Lectionary* is used for the proclamation of the first and second reading and often for the psalm. The *Gospel Book* is used for the proclamation of the gospel. During less solemn liturgies, such as a daily Mass, the gospel may also be proclaimed from the *Lectionary*.

The *Missal*, or *Roman Missal*, formerly known as the *Sacramentary*, is the third book used for the celebration of the Eucharist. This book contains all the prayers for the Mass and is used exclusively by the celebrant of the Mass to lead the assembly in prayer. It is not a symbol of Christ, so it is never carried in procession.

In addition to these three books used for the celebration of the Eucharist, all other sacraments and rituals—such as the Order of Christian Initiation of Adults, the Order of Holy Matrimony, Sunday Celebrations in the Absence of a Priest, and the Order of Christian Funerals, to name a few—have their own proper books.

Easter Fire

Fire is among the most powerful primary symbols. Throughout history, bonfires have been lit during small family gatherings as well as for large public celebrations. In pre-Christian times, Europeans built big bonfires at the time of the summer solstice and winter solstice and the spring equinox and fall equinox. Although the specific purpose of these fires is unknown, it is likely related to light and darkness and good and evil. Fires were lit to ward off evil, symbolized by darkness, while the fire itself

symbolized light and goodness. A fire lit at night was a powerful symbol of the light breaking through the darkness.

Christians adopted this symbolic way of warding off evil and darkness but gave it a Christian meaning. The Christian version of the fire marking the summer solstice is known as the St. John's fire. The fire is lit on the eve of the celebration of the birth of St. John the Baptist on June 24, when the days begin to shorten. St. John is the one who foretold the coming of the Savior, the Light of the World. As the light begins to fade after the longest day of the year, the St. John's fire points to the shortest day of the year, at the winter solstice, when we celebrate the birth of Jesus, the Light that never fades.

The winter solstice bonfire became the Epiphany fire. In many countries, Christians bring their Christmas trees to a common place for a communal celebration of Epiphany, marked by the burning of these trees. Christmas lights and candles on trees also symbolize that light breaks through the darkness. Neither the St. John's fire nor the Epiphany fire made their way into the official liturgical life of the Church, but it was customary for the local priest to bless these fires.

The fire lit at the spring equinox became the Easter fire and was incorporated into the Easter Vigil. For Christians, the Easter fire symbolizes that Jesus Christ is the Light of the World who broke through the darkness once and for all. The Easter candle, or paschal candle, is lit from the Easter fire during the Easter Vigil.

Holy Oils and the Ambry

Three kinds of blessed oil are used in the sacramental life of the church: the oil of catechumens (*oleum catechumenorum*, or OC), the oil of the sick (*oleum infirmorum*, or OI), and the sacred chrism (*sanctum chrisma*, or SC). The vessels containing these oils are often marked with the letters OC, OI, or SC to distinguish between the oils. All three oils are blessed by the bishop during the chrism Mass, which is traditionally celebrated on the morning of Holy Thursday to ready the new oils for the Easter Vigil. Today, the chrism Mass is often celebrated earlier in Holy Week or even in the weeks leading up to Holy Week to allow for greater attendance.

The oil of catechumens may be used on one or on several occasions for adults who are preparing to be initiated into the Catholic Church. This anointing follows a prayer of exorcism. Because of this, St. Hippolytus in 215 referred to this oil as the oil of exorcism. In the same way wrestlers use oil to prepare their bodies for the task at hand, catechumens are anointed with the oil of catechumens to be spiritually prepared for their initiation and strengthened on their journey to the font. Infants who are baptized may also be anointed with the oil of catechumens before being baptized. Anointing children with the oil of catechumens is done because infant baptism is based on adult initiation, which comprises many rites over an extended period, including anointing with the oil of catechumens. Still, like adults, children also need strength for their faith journey ahead, and their anointing with the oil of catechumens accomplishes just that.

The oil of the sick is used for the sacrament of anointing of the sick. This symbol clearly relies on the healing power inherent in oil. As oil soothes the skin, we pray that it may do the same to the body, spirit, and soul of the sick person being anointed. The sacrament of the sick was known as extreme unction before the Second Vatican Council and was administered only when a person was in danger of dying. Now, the sacrament with the anointing is celebrated whenever a person is gravely ill but not necessarily in danger of death.

Sacred chrism is used during infant baptism, at confirmation, for the ordination of bishops and priests, and when dedicating an altar and a church. In all these cases, the oil symbolizes the imparting of the power of the Holy Spirit associated with each specific sacrament. As the oil penetrates the skin, we pray that the Spirit may consecrate the person or the object that is anointed. The word "chrism" is derived from the Greek verb that means "to anoint." Sacred chrism is scented with balsam, a sweet aromatic perfume used since ancient times. This makes the experience of being anointed not only tactile but also olfactory. This is in reference St. Paul's words to the Corinthians: "For we are the aroma of Christ for God among those who are being saved and among those who are perishing, to the latter an odor of death that leads to death, to the former an odor of life that leads to life. Who is qualified for this?" (2 Corinthians 2:15–16).

The sacred oils are reserved in a container called an *ambry*. This name is derived from two Latin words: *almarium*, which means "a chest for storage," and *armarium*, which means "a chest for tools or arms." Sacred oils are our spiritual tools or arms. The ambry, a solid metal box that is recessed into the wall, has traditionally been located either in the sanctuary or in the sacristy. The words *Olea Sancta* or "Holy Oils" may be inscribed on the locked door.

In newer churches, the sacred oils are given a more prominent and visible place. Because of the connection between two of the oils with the sacraments of initiation, the ambry is best located near the baptismal font. Contemporary ambries often incorporate glass to allow the different oils to be seen.

Chalice and Paten

Two of the most recognizable and important liturgical objects are the chalice and the paten that are used for the celebration of the Eucharist. The word "chalice" comes from the Latin word *calix*, which in turn comes from the

Greek word *kylix*, "a cup raised on a foot or base." The word "paten" comes from the Latin *patina*, or "shallow dish," which in turn comes from the Greek *patane*, or "plate." The paten contains the bread that becomes the Body of Christ during the Eucharist, and the chalice contains the wine that becomes the Blood of Christ. The chalice is first among the sacred vessels because it is synonymous with the Precious Blood of Christ. In St. Paul's first Letter to the Corinthians, he wrote, "The cup of blessing that we bless, is it not a participation in the Blood of Christ?" (1 Corinthians 10:16).

The first versions of the chalice and paten were undoubtedly whatever was used by the community to eat and drink, and they may have been made of glass, pottery, ivory, or metal. One of the earliest mentions of chalices made from precious metal and decorated with jewels was during a homily preached by St. John Chrysostom (347–407).

Given the scarcity of vessels, it was common to share the same cup among those dining together. This was the custom at the time of the Last Supper, when Jesus took the cup and gave it to his disciples, saying, "This cup is the new covenant in my blood. Do this, as often as you drink it, in remembrance of me" (1 Corinthians 11:25).

Depictions of chalices in early Christian art reveal an almost stemless, vase-shaped type with two handles. These were relatively large, because there was one chalice to be shared by all. While drinking directly from the chalice was common, a fibula or golden straw was used in some places. Incidentally, this is still one of the approved ways of receiving the Precious Blood.

Already in the fifth century, a distinction was made between the clergy and the assembly in terms of receiving from the cup. In some places, this was manifested in using a separate chalice for clergy and laity. A smaller chalice was used by the priest to facilitate the elevation of the chalice after the consecration. In other places, the chalice was withheld from the laity, mostly out of fear of spilling the Precious Blood. Although Pope St. Leo the Great (440–461) and others had declared withholding the cup from the laity a heresy, the practice of reserving the cup for the priest began to appear again in the eleventh century and quickly grew in popularity. It was declared the official practice of the Catholic Church in 1415 at the Council of Constance. The restoration of reception under both species for everyone happened after the Second Vatican Council.

The creation of a separate chalice for the priest and the withholding of the chalice from the laity resulted in a redesign of the chalice. The bowl containing the wine became much smaller, as just a little wine was needed. The stem of the cup became taller to make it easier to elevate the chalice after the consecration. A knob in the middle of the stem was added to allow steadier holding of the chalice. The base also became broader to offer more stability to the top-heavy chalice.

The paten also evolved over time as the bread morphed into hosts and Communion by the faithful became rare. The once-large paten became just large enough to hold the host of the priest only. The chalice and paten are often made of the same material, with related decorations, and the paten is shaped so that it can sit easily on the chalice.

Since the restoration of Communion under both species, there is often a principal chalice used by the ordained ministers, while several smaller cups are used for the distribution of the Precious Blood to the assembly. Though we commune from different cups, the principal cup symbolizes our unity in the Blood of Christ.

Monstrance

A monstrance is an elaborately decorated object that is designed to hold the consecrated host during exposition of the Blessed Sacrament, adoration, benediction, and processions with the Blessed Sacrament. The word "monstrance" comes from the Latin verb *monstrare,* meaning "to show." Originally, a monstrance could be created to hold either a relic of a saint or the consecrated host. Today, the word "monstrance" is used to refer exclusively to a vessel designed to hold the Blessed Sacrament. Similar vessels designed to hold relics of the saints are called reliquaries. A monstrance is also known as an "ostensorium" from the Latin *ostendere* which also means "to show" or "to display."

The earliest monstrances were mostly tower-like, and they did not have a crystal inset to allow the host to be seen, because the need to see the host for veneration did not yet exist. A fully exposed host did not become the norm for adoration until after the Council of Trent in the second half of the sixteenth century.

The desire to see the host dictated a complete redesign of the monstrance. The base is usually rather broad, to assure stability. The stem is tall and has a knob in the middle to allow for easier handling. An aureole or sunburst is the main part of the monstrance and sits on the stem. In the middle of the aureole is the crystal container that holds and reveals the consecrated host. When the host is displayed in the monstrance, it is first placed between two circular glass plates connected by precious metal that is known as the *luna,* from the Latin for "moon." The luna keeps the host in place in the monstrance so that it is secured with the reverence it is due. A monstrance is often richly decorated, sometimes embedded with precious stones.

Ciborium

A ciborium is made to hold the consecrated hosts that are reserved in the tabernacle. The name is Latin in origin but is derived from the Greek *kiborion,* meaning "a cup-shaped vessel." Its shape, therefore, is often like that of a chalice, although the cup of the ciborium is wider so that it can hold more hosts. Because a ciborium holds the Body of Christ, it is made of precious metal, either gilded silver or gold. A ciborium has a lid to better protect the consecrated hosts that are reserved in it. The lid is dome-shaped to accommodate more hosts.

The top of the lid is often decorated with a cross or a small globe topped with a cross. In addition to the theological implications, this has a very practical purpose: to allow for easy removal of the lid. Modern ciboriums come in many different forms that may not resemble the cup after which it is named.

In the past, a ciborium was covered with a ciborium veil before it was placed in the tabernacle. Though no longer used in many churches, this veil consisted of a piece of cloth in the shape of a Greek cross, with the four arms of the cross being the same length, and with a small slit in the center. The cross on top of the ciborium cover was placed through the slit, thus allowing the four sides of the cross-shaped veil to cover the ciborium.

Incense and Thurible

The use of incense in the liturgy can be traced to ancient Jewish temple rituals and Roman imperial court practices. The word "incense" comes from the Latin verb *incendere,* meaning "to burn." In the Christian liturgy, incense is placed on burning coals to release both smoke and aroma. The use of incense augments our visual and olfactory participation in the celebration of the liturgy.

In the same way as incense was burnt as an offering in supplication to God in the Hebrew Scriptures, we, too, burn incense as a symbol of the prayers we offer. In the Book of Psalms, it reads, "Let my prayer be incense before you; my uplifted hands an evening offering" (Psalm 141:2).

In addition, we use incense to honor the presence of Christ in the Eucharist as well as the different liturgical symbols of Christ, such as the altar, the *Gospel Book*, the priest, the people of God, the cross, and the Easter candle. When we honor these symbols of Christ with incense, we honor Christ himself.

Different types of incense can be used to mark the different liturgical seasons. In that way, incense helps distinguish between the seasons not only visually and acoustically but also olfactorily.

In the Catholic Church, incense is burnt in a thurible. The word "thurible" comes from the Latin *thuribulum,* which shares a root with the Greek verb *thuein*, meaning "to sacrifice." The basic shape of the thurible is a metal bowl with enough room for at least one coal and a perforated cover that allows the incense to billow out through the holes. At least one chain, if not several, holds the bowl and the cover together and allows the thurible to be swung. An incense boat, which holds the incense and is imposed on the coals during the liturgy, is usually made to match the thurible. Incense is carried by the thurifer, or bearer of the thurible, at the beginning of solemn processions.

One very dramatic use of incense is during the blessing of a new altar. After the altar has been anointed with sacred chrism, a large vessel is placed on the altar, and copious amounts of incense are placed on the coals contained in the vessel.

A well-known example of a thurible is the

Botafumeiro that is used in the Cathedral of Santiago de Compostela in Spain. It is suspended from the ceiling, weighs 117 pounds, is 5 feet tall, and, when swung using a system of ropes, can reach up to 42 miles per hour.

Holy Water Stoops and Founts

When I was growing up, my siblings and I each had a small holy water stoop—an ornate, cup-like container—attached to the wall next to the door frame inside our bedrooms. We received these containers as a gift at our baptisms. The first thing we did upon entering our rooms was dip our fingers into the holy water and bless ourselves. Then, we said a prayer, and only after that were we allowed to go to bed. The custom of a holy water stoop inside a bedroom is rare today, and rarer is the custom to bless ourselves before going to sleep or at any other time for that matter. The liturgy, however, has preserved several forms of blessing, including blessing with holy water, which is one of the most popular sacramentals we have.

The sacrament of baptism is the sacrament by which we become part of the body of Christ: the Church. It is the first sacrament; without it, no other sacrament can be celebrated. Given that baptism is considered the fundamental sacrament, it is appropriate to reference this sacrament during the celebration of any other sacraments, whether through verbal acknowledgment or symbolic representation. At certain times, the liturgy references our rootedness in baptism very explicitly, such as at the beginning of a funeral Mass. Whenever possible, the body of the deceased or the cremated remains are placed near the baptismal font during the wake or visitation. At the beginning of the service, the liturgical ministers meet the family members gathered around the coffin or urn at the entrance of the church. This is a reference to the time when the family of the deceased brought him or her to church for baptism. Then, too, they were met at the doors of the church by the priest. The remains of the deceased are then sprinkled with holy water in remembrance of the deceased's baptism. When the body is present, a pall, or white cloth, is placed over the coffin as a reference to the baptismal gown the deceased was wearing at the time of baptism.

Another example is the sprinkling rite, which may be used in lieu of the penitential rite at the beginning of Mass. The sprinkling rite as a reminder of our baptism is particularly meaningful during the season of Easter, with its initiatory character.

Maybe less explicit but in no way less meaningful is the custom of blessing ourselves when we enter church. Though this may have become routine and be done without much thought, it is nonetheless a powerful reminder of our baptism and the rights and obligations that come with it. What better place to remind ourselves of our baptism than at the baptismal font. New and remodeled churches often have large baptismal fonts near the entrance of the church. Their size and location alone make it clear that baptism is indeed the first of the sacraments. In these churches, the font also functions as the place where people go to bless themselves upon entering the church.

Before the Second Vatican Council, baptismal fonts were hidden in baptismal chapels with locked doors, which made it impossible for a font to be used outside of baptism. Small holy water founts or stoops were located at every door of the church, so that the faithful could have easy access to holy water. Sometimes, these founts were elaborately decorated, such as those at Saint Peter's Basilica in Rome. These small hand founts are not seen often in contemporary churches, as current practice favors the fuller symbol of blessing oneself with holy water from the baptismal font.

Tower Bells

When I first moved to the United States, I was struck by the absence of the sound of bells. Growing up in Belgium, we were surrounded by the sound of bells, especially on Sunday mornings, when the churches in town announced the beginning of Mass.

For centuries, Catholic churches have used bells to communicate with the broader community. In a sense, bells are the voice of the church. Bells announced joyous occasions, such as baptisms, weddings, or liturgical festivals. They were used to signal disasters, summon people to worship, and indicate the time of day, such as morning, midday, and evening. A church's bells would ring to announce that someone in the parish had died. The tower bells were rung in different configurations and patterns, and the people knew what each one meant.

Traditionally, bells were "baptized." They were given the name of a saint, symbolizing that when the bells rang, the saint was calling people to church. They were washed with holy water and consecrated with sacred chrism. Today, bells are no longer baptized. They are given names, and they are blessed, and the current blessing is beautiful and speaks to their meaning.

Lord, from the beginning of time, your
voice has called to us,
inviting us to communion with you,
teaching us the mysteries of your life,
guiding us on the way to salvation.
With silver trumpets, Moses summoned
Israel to gather as your people.
Now you are pleased that in the Church,
the sound of bells should summon your
people in prayer.

By this blessing, accept these bells into your service.
May their voice direct our hearts toward you
and prompt us to come gladly to this church,
there to experience the presence of Christ,
listen to your word, offer you our prayers,
and, both in joy and in sorrow, be friends to one another.
Through Christ our Lord. Amen

One specific way church bells are used is as an invitation to pray the Angelus. Whereas monastics and clerics pray many times during the day, and their prayers are rather lengthy, the Angelus is a shortened version prayed by the faithful in the morning, at midday and in the evening. The name *Angelus* is the first word of the Latin version of the Angelus prayer: *Angelus Domini nuntiavit Mariæ* or "The Angel of the Lord declared to Mary." The Angelus prayer honors the moment when the Angel Gabriel announced to Mary that she would conceive and bear a son. The Angelus bells ring in a specific pattern of three times three with a pause in between each set of three, followed by festive swinging of a bell. The traditional prayer goes as follows:

The Angel of the Lord declared to Mary:
And she conceived of the Holy Spirit.
Hail Mary...
Behold the handmaid of the Lord:
Be it done unto me according to thy word.
Hail Mary...
And the Word was made flesh:
And dwelt among us.
Hail Mary...
Pray for us, O Holy Mother of God,
that we may be made worthy of the promises of Christ.
Let us pray:
Pour forth, we beseech thee, O Lord, thy grace into our hearts; that we, to whom the incarnation of Christ, thy Son, was made known by the message of an angel, may by his passion and cross be brought to the glory of his resurrection, through the same Christ our Lord.
Amen.

The Sanctus bells, or altar bells, are a set of handheld bells that were rung during Mass at the end of the Sanctus, or Holy, Holy, Holy, and at the time of the elevation of the Body and Blood of Christ during the consecration. These bells were used at a time when the participation of the faithful in the Mass was minimal. The celebration of the Mass was the prerogative of the clergy, while the faithful were engaged in devotional practices. The Sanctus bells were rung to draw attention to the consecration and to invite the faithful to gaze upon the Body and

Blood of Christ during the elevations at a time when ocular, or visual, Communion was more popular than actual Communion.

The ringing of the Sanctus bells was formally mandated by the Council of Trent (1545–1563). Today, it is no longer required, though in some churches the Sanctus bells are rung to emphasize the sacredness of the consecration.

Liturgical Linens: Corporal, Purificator, and Burse

In addition to the altar cloth, which covers the altar, several liturgical linens are used during the celebration of the Mass.

A corporal is a square, white linen cloth that is placed on the altar cloth during the preparation of the altar and the gifts. The chalice and paten are placed on the corporal. The corporal is intended to honor the Body and Blood of Christ as well as to catch any particles of the host that might fall. At the end of Communion, after the purification rite, the corporal is folded in such a way that it encloses any fallen particles of the host. When not in use, the corporal was traditionally placed in a burse, or corporal case. Though the corporal is still used, the use of a burse is less common today.

A purificator is a white piece of cloth that is used to wipe the rim of a chalice after people receive holy Communion. It is also used during the purification rite to wipe the chalice dry.

Faithful Reflections

There are many liturgical symbols used for the celebration of our sacraments. We might recognize them by sight, but we might not know their names, what they are used for, where they are from, or what they mean. The next time you go to church, take some time to look around—really look around—and think about the objects and furnishings you see that are used to celebrate the sacraments. Look at them carefully, think about them, and meditate on them.

- *Do you have any special dishes at home? Maybe they belonged to a favorite aunt. Or you may have purchased them in a place that is special to you. What makes them so special, and how do you use them differently from other dishes? What can these plates in your home teach you about the vessels used in liturgy?*
- *What do the liturgical objects in your church look like? What do they express? What do they tell you?*
- *How is incense used to honor Christ's presence in your church? What are other ways to honor Christ's presence? How can you honor Christ's presence in your home, where you work, and with your friends in daily living?*

CHAPTER SEVEN

The Symbolic Meaning of Liturgical Garb

A New York friend told me about a woman who would approach him each day to beg for money while he was having lunch in a park. Although she said nothing, she would walk by and extend her hand toward him, then wait for him to give her money. The woman stood out from the other people in the park because she was wearing a full nun's habit, including a wimple that covered her neck and head. After several weeks, doubting the woman was an actual nun, my friend finally told her it was rude to impersonate a nun to get money. Without missing a beat, she replied, "I never told you I was a nun!" And, in truth, she had not, at least not in so many words. However, the clothing she wore told us otherwise, and it is hard to imagine that making people believe she was a nun was not her intent.

Certain types of clothing tell a story or imply a profession. People who wear scrubs are associated with a medical setting. Police officers, firefighters, and other first responders are recognized by the uniforms they wear. Ordained ministers are easily recognized by their clerical collars, though their denominational affiliation may be unclear. A person wearing a ring, pectoral cross, miter, and crosier is undoubtedly a bishop. Clothing has a practical purpose but is sometimes laden with symbolism.

The Roman Catholic Church has a long tradition of liturgical vestments, most of which have their origins in the daily dress of the Roman Empire. Although the specifics of who can wear what for which services is clearly defined today, liturgical garb was ruled for centuries by local custom. It was not until the thirteenth century that Church law began to regulate what should be worn at Mass. Our current *Code of Canon Law* devotes several paragraphs to liturgical vesture.

The purpose of wearing special garb for the celebration of the liturgy is twofold. First, it allows the congregation to differentiate between the different ministers, because laypeople, deacons, priests, and bishops all wear different dress. Second, vestments add solemnity to the celebration and indicate what liturgical season and what type of liturgy is being celebrated, because vestments differ for various liturgical seasons and celebrations.

THOUGH THE SYMBOLIC MEANING OF VESTMENTS IS PRIMARILY DRAWN FROM THEIR FORM, SHAPE, AND COLOR, SOMETIMES OTHER SYMBOLS ARE ADDED TO VESTMENTS TO ENHANCE THEIR CONNECTION WITH PARTICULAR FEASTS OR SEASONS.

Vestments are distinguished from one another by their shape, their color, and sometimes by the decorations that are applied to the vestments. The colors used for vestments follow the colors of the liturgical year. As such, the color violet is used for the preparatory season of Advent and the penitential season of Lent. The color rose is worn on two days of the year: the third Sunday of Advent and the fourth Sunday of Lent. These Sundays are respectively known as Gaudete Sunday and Laetare Sunday, after the first word of the Introit, or entrance song, for the Mass on those days. White is used principally for the seasons of Christmas and Easter and for other solemnities and certain feasts. In the United States, silver and gold may be used in lieu of or to augment white vestments. Green is used for Ordinary Time, and red is used on Palm Sunday, Good Friday, Pentecost, and on the feast days of martyrs.

Violet is used for the preparatory season of Advent and the penitential season of Lent.

Rose is worn on two days of the year: the third Sunday of Advent and the fourth Sunday of Lent/

White is used principally for the seasons of Christmas and Easter and for other solemnities and certain feasts.

Green is used for Ordinary Time.

Red is used on Palm Sunday, Good Friday, Pentecost, and on the feast days of martyrs.

The color of vestment is also dependent on the sacrament that is celebrated, regardless of the liturgical season. White is worn for weddings and also for funerals, although violet or black, the color for funerals before the Second Vatican Council, may also be used. Red is worn at confirmations when they are not celebrated on Sunday or certain solemnities that dictate another liturgical color.

Though the symbolic meaning of vestments is primarily drawn from their form, shape, and color, sometimes other symbols are added to vestments to enhance their connection with particular feasts or seasons. These details always need to be approached with care and moderation so that any images added to a liturgical vestment do not obscure the main symbol, which is the garment itself.

Monastic Habit

A habit is a generic term for the type of garb worn by members of religious orders and monastic communities. This is not their liturgical vesture but their day-to-day garb. Habits come in different materials, shapes, and colors, which help in identifying the religious order of the wearer. The word "habit" comes from the Latin *habitus*, meaning "condition," "bearing," "state," "appearance," "dress," and "attire." A habit not only signifies the wearer's commitment to simplicity of life, prayer, and service, it also is intended to assist in living out these virtues.

A habit has different parts, often including a tunic, a belt, and a scapular. The tunic is the base garment, which is gathered at the waist by a belt. A scapular consists of two large pieces of cloth that are worn front and back over the shoulders and sometimes has a hood. The term "scapular" comes from the Latin *scapula*, meaning "shoulder." In certain orders, women and men who have made their solemn professions wear a pleated oversized cowl, or *cuculla*, during the celebration of the liturgy. The Latin word *cuculla* means "hood" or "cowl." For example, the cowl of the Benedictines has seventy-three pleats, one for each chapter of the *Rule of Saint Benedict*. In addition to all this, women of religious orders often wear a veil that covers their hair.

The greatest difference in habits of religious orders is the color. The habit of Benedictines is black. Dominicans wear all white. Franciscans wear brown with a rope instead of a belt. Cistercians wear white habits and black scapulars. Some orders are more colorful in their selections; for example, members of the Order of the Most Holy Annunciation, also known as the "Blue Nuns," wear bright blue habits.

Laypeople do not wear habits, but there is a type of scapular—a devotional scapular—that may be worn by laypeople. The devotional scapular consists of two small squares that are attached to one another with a ribbon, and it is worn over the shoulders under one's outer clothing. There are different types of devotional scapulars. The most popular is the Brown scapular, which according to tradition, was handed to the prior general of the Carmelite Order, St. Simon Stock, at Aylesford, England, during an apparition of the Blessed Mother in 1251. Wearing the scapular implies a Marian devotion and is a reminder of her protection. It is believed that a person who wears this scapular when dying will be saved from hell and released from purgatory on the first Saturday after death, known as the Sabbatine Privilege. The wearing of the Brown scapular became very popular in the sixteenth and seventeenth centuries due to support and promotion by several popes. For a long time, a Brown scapular was given to a child at baptism.

Clerical Cassock

Diocesan priests and bishops do not usually wear habits because most of them do not belong to monastic or religious communities. Instead of habits, they have traditionally worn cassocks. "Cassock" comes from the Middle French *casaque*, meaning "long coat." It is also known as a "soutane," from the Latin *subtus*, meaning "beneath." A soutane is indeed worn beneath liturgical vestments.

Though there are variations, a typical Roman cassock is a long tunic with buttons in the front from top to bottom. A sash is often worn around the waist. The color of the cassock is dictated by the clerical state of the wearer. Priests wear black, although in tropical climates, they may wear white. While most priests wore cassocks before the Second Vatican Council, today the cassock has been largely replaced by a black suit and shirt with a white Roman collar. The house cassock of a bishop has purple piping, while his liturgical cassock is entirely purple. The house cassock of a cardinal has red piping, while their liturgical cassock is entirely red. The cassock of the pope is entirely white.

Attire of the Assembly

Although many people have become rather informal in their selection of clothes in general, they still opt to wear certain types of clothes to certain types of events. Different clothes are worn to a baseball game than to a picnic, even though both are casual events. Likewise, varying degrees of formal dress are seen when attending a fine dinner or church. Clothes not only dress the body but communicate, knowingly or not, how wearers feel about the event they attend. I remember giving a talk in Green Bay

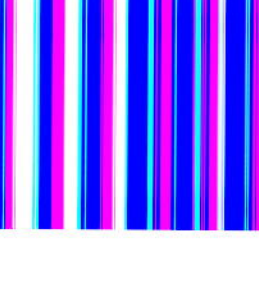

during Lent. I decided to wear a purple tie to honor the color of the liturgical season of Lent. This ended up being a poor choice in the city of the Green Bay Packers. People were convinced that I intentionally had worn purple, the color of their archrivals, the Minnesota Vikings. No explanation could persuade them otherwise.

The way a person dresses is of course a very personal and delicate matter. Still, there is appropriate and inappropriate dress for worship. Noone wants to hear that his or her outfit is inappropriate for church, so a good question to ask before leaving for church is, "Do my clothes speak to the importance of the celebration of the Eucharist?" If not, then it is best to wear something else. Also ask yourself, "Will what I am wearing distract others from their prayer and worship?" If so, then it is best to wear something else. Everything associated with the liturgy must underline the importance of the celebration and support the celebration. This includes our attire.

Alb

The most common and basic of all liturgical vestments is the alb, a white garment that reaches down to the ankles. The word "alb" is derived from the Latin word *albis,* which means "white." This is the one piece of vesture that may be worn by ordained and lay ministers alike. All of us wear it by virtue of our baptism, as it harkens back to our baptismal gown. It does not denote any specific ministry in the church.

The origin of the alb is found in the simple Roman tunic. Like all liturgical vesture, it has been made of various materials with different decorative elements throughout its history. Today's albs are usually very simple in style and material, although some use more traditional albs that are trimmed with lace at the bottom and around the sleeves. Hooded albs are traditionally reserved for monks. The white hood is intended to cover the black or brown hood that is part of a monk's habit.

An alb is the foundational liturgical garment worn beneath most other garments that ordained ministers wear. If an ordained minister wears a cassock or a habit, then an alb is worn over it.

A shorter variant of the alb is the surplice. This is the white garment worn over the cassock by some altar servers and some members of the clergy. A surplice is often made from linen and is simple in style, although, depending on the taste of the wearer, it may be adorned with lace at the bottom and around the sleeves.

Stole

A stole is a narrow band of colored textile, often silk or wool, that is worn by ordained ministers. The word "stole" comes from the Latin *stola,* which means "garment." During Roman times, the *stola* served as a kind of wide, ample scarf that was worn by men and women alike, wrapped generously around their shoulders to keep them warm. Gradually, the *stola* worn by men during liturgy became narrow and a marker of a specific ordained ministry.

Today, there are two different kinds of stoles: one style for deacons and another for priests and bishops. The deacon's stole is worn over the left shoulder and gathered at the waist on the right. The stole is worn over an alb, and under a dalmatic or cope when these are worn. A priest wears the stole around his neck, over the alb, and under the chasuble or cope when they are worn. Stoles that are worn under other garments are often simpler and lighter than those worn over the alb without additional vestments. The color of the stole depends on the liturgical feast or season.

Dalmatic

A dalmatic is a vestment worn by deacons during the celebration of the Eucharist or other appropriate liturgical functions. It is worn over the alb and stole. Like all liturgical garb, it has its origin in the Roman Empire, where it was worn as a form of secular clothing. By the fourth century, however, the dalmatic was firmly established as a liturgical vestment.

The dalmatic is a simple square tunic with wide sleeves. Today, the sides are usually sown closed, but examples still exist of dalmatics that are open on the sides and worn as a garment similar to the way a scapular is worn over the habit of members of religious communities.

The color of the dalmatic depends on the liturgical season or celebration. The use of additional symbols or decorative elements, which may refer to the sacraments celebrated by the deacon wearing them, should be sparing, because the dalmatic communicates primarily by virtue of its shape and color.

Chasuble

The chasuble is worn for the celebration of the Eucharist by priests and bishops. This vestment, too, has its origins in a Roman secular garment that was most often worn for traveling. It was appropriately named *casula*, a word that means "little house," illustrating the fact that a chasuble covers almost the entire person. The original *casula* was a large circular piece of cloth with a hole in the center. It was pulled over the head, like an oversized poncho, and

reached nearly to the ground. The *casula* needed to be gathered up to reveal hands and arms.

As the use of the chasuble in the liturgy became more popular, it was adapted to fit the needs of the celebration of the Eucharist. First, the sides were made shorter to free up the hands, resulting in what looked more like an oversized bib rather than a poncho, and certainly not a *casula*. The sides became even shorter and disappeared altogether in the sixteenth century to allow a priest to more easily elevate the Eucharist above his head. He had to do this because he was celebrating the Mass with his back to the people, who needed to be able to view the consecrated Eucharist during the elevation. This type of chasuble is known as the "fiddleback" because it is shaped like a violin. Today's chasubles resemble the original shape of the *casula* more closely and are made of more ample material.

Like other vestments, chasubles follow the colors of the liturgical seasons and celebrations. They are often made out of wool, silk, or other natural materials. Although chasubles throughout history have been heavily decorated with symbols or augmented with abstract or decorative designs, today's chasubles principally rely on color and fabric to suggest the liturgical days and time of year and are much simpler in their expression.

Cope

Bishops, priests, and deacons wear a cope for liturgical celebrations other than the celebration of the Eucharist, such as during exposition of the Blessed Sacrament or weddings that do not include the Eucharist. The word "cope" is rooted in the Latin word *cappa*, meaning "cape." Not surprisingly, the cope is a large cape that is open in the front, held together with a clasp, and reaches to the ground.

Except for the elimination of a hood, the cope has not changed much in shape since its earliest liturgical use as far back as the sixth century. At that time, the hood had a very practical purpose, which was to protect its wearer from sun or rain during outdoor processions. Gradually, the hood became an ornamental element and shifted into the back panel, as is seen on many copes from the Middle Ages. This panel was often richly embroidered with Christian symbols or images of saints and decorated with fringes and a tassel. Today's copes are much simpler than their medieval counterparts and usually do not include the back panel or symbolic decorative elements.

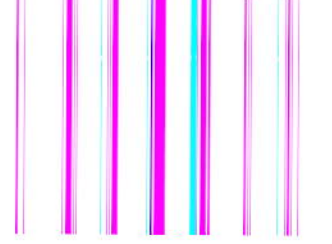

Humeral Veil

The humeral veil is worn only during Benediction of the Blessed Sacrament and during processions with the Blessed Sacrament. It is a long, rectangular piece of cloth held together by a clasp, used by an ordained minister when holding the monstrance or sometimes the ciborium.

The term "humeral veil," or "shoulder veil," comes from the Latin *humerus,* meaning "shoulder." The humeral veil is usually about six to eight feet long and one and a half feet wide. Pockets are sown into the inside of each side of the veil so the user may slip his hands into them to more easily hold the monstrance or ciborium.

The origin of this veil goes back to the Roman imperial custom of servants being ready with a similar veil, known as the *sudarium,* to hold whatever object might be handed to them. This practice implies that the servant is unworthy to touch the object directly. The wearing of the humeral veil by an ordained minister emphasizes the sacredness of the Blessed Sacrament being carried or raised.

Miter

The miter is the pointed hat worn by bishops and abbots during certain parts of the celebration of the liturgy. The word is derived from the Greek *mitra,* which means "headband." The miter seems to have originated from the headdress worn by officials in the Roman imperial court. When the bishop of Rome adopted this garment, it was not intended for liturgical use at first, but rather as an outdoor garment. It became a liturgical garment when he wore it during solemn processions. By the tenth century, he also wore it during indoor liturgies. It would take about another 100 years for bishops across the Christian West to wear a miter.

The first universal type of miter was a curved rounded cap with an ornamental band. Sometimes, it had a depression in the middle. References to the current shape of the miter date to the beginning of the twelfth century. It consists of two pointed panels sewn together with two cloth flaps, called *lappets*, in the back.

Crosier

The crosier, or pastoral staff, carried by bishops is another one of the insignia of the office of the bishop. It is inspired by the shepherd's custom of carrying a crook when shepherding his flock, and it symbolizes the jurisdiction and authority of the bishop in his diocese. It is carried in processions and held during specific liturgical acts, such as preaching or confirmation. Bishops can only use their crosier within their own diocese except with explicit permission from the local bishop.

Though the crosier was likely used earlier, it was clearly documented for the first time at the Council of Toledo in 633. Crosiers can be made from any material, ranging from wood to precious metals. They can be very simple, with minimal decoration, or very elaborate. Most bishops today opt for simpler crosiers.

The Roman Catholic Church has two types of crosier. The most popular version is shaped like a shepherd's hook. The second version, known as a *ferula*, meaning "rod" or "staff," is a staff with a small orb on top that is surmounted by a large cross. The use of a *ferula* is principally, though not exclusively, reserved for the pope. A well-known *ferula* commissioned by Pope St. Paul VI from Italian sculptor Lello Scorzelli in 1963 has a corpus on the cross, which broke with tradition. His successors used the same *ferula*, though Pope Benedict XVI started using a more traditional *ferula* in 2008. Like the late Pope Francis, Pope Leo XIV seems to favor the *ferula* of Pope St. Paul VI.

A crosier is not to be confused with an archiepiscopal or patriarchal cross, which is a cross with two horizontal bars: one in addition to the usual one. Archbishops have the privilege of an archiepiscopal cross, which may be carried in procession before them and should not be used as crosier. This is more akin to a processional cross rather than to a crosier.

Pectoral Cross

Many people wear a small cross around their neck. They might wear it as a decorative necklace to testify to their faith or inside their shirt as a form of protection. A pectoral cross, however, is much larger and worn only by certain people to show their ecclesiastical rank. As such, the pectoral cross is worn by bishops, abbots, and abbesses.

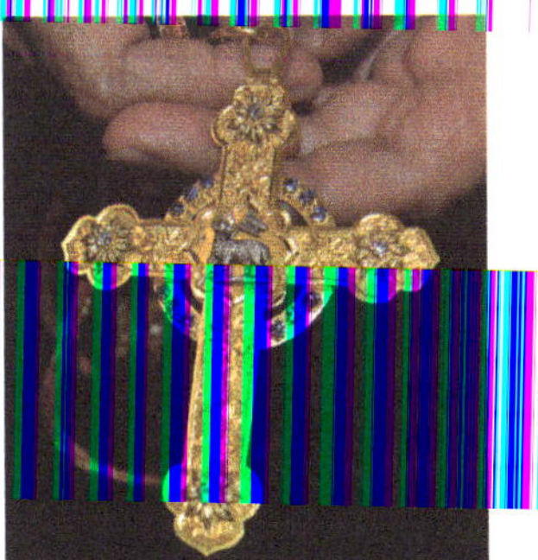

The name for the "pectoral" cross comes from the Latin word *pectoralis*, meaning "chest." Not surprisingly, the pectoral cross is worn hanging from a chain or rope over the heart or the chest. The style of a pectoral cross can range from very simple to complex. The cross can be made from unadorned wood or metal set with precious or semi-precious stones.

During the liturgy, the pectoral cross is worn above the bishop's vestments and hangs from a green and white braided rope with a tassel on the back. The colors of this braided rope for a cardinal are gold and red.

Ring

When he is consecrated, a bishop receives a ring in addition to the other symbols of his office, such as the miter and the crosier. The origin of the bishop's ring might lie in the fact that documents at the time of early Christianity were sealed with the ring of the holder of the office that issued the document. The seal of the ring validated the document. After the death of a pope, his ring was immediately destroyed so no more documents could be sealed with his ring.

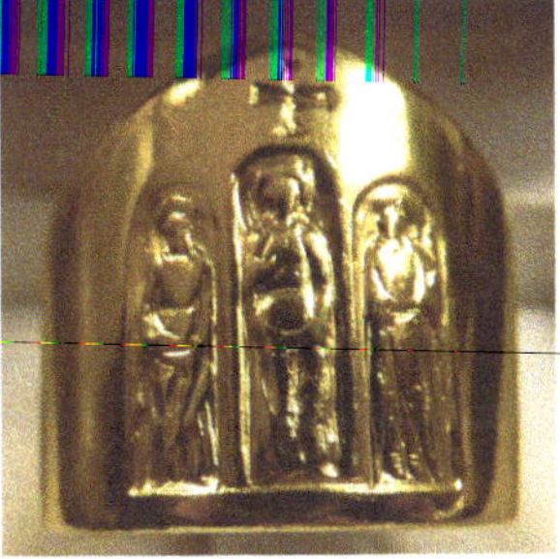

Bishops no longer validate documents with their rings. The bishop's ring now has a much more symbolic meaning that shows the supreme loyalty of the bishop to Christ and his Church, like the union between two spouses expressed by a wedding ring.

The insignia of Abbots and Abbesses

Abbots and abbesses, the elected leaders of monastic communities, have the right to wear a ring and pectoral cross, which are usually associated with the office of a bishop. Because the crosier is the symbol of authority and jurisdiction within a specific territory, abbots and some abbesses who have authority over their respective communities are given a crosier. In addition to a crosier, an abbot also may wear a miter when presiding over the liturgy in his own abbey. Abbesses do not receive a miter because their liturgical roles are different from those of their male counterparts and do not merit a miter. Some medieval abbesses did have the right both to a miter and crosier. These were not often worn by the abbess but usually carried behind her in procession.

Pallium

A pallium is worn by the pope and by metropolitan archbishops who preside over an ecclesiastical province comprised of several surrounding dioceses. Its liturgical usage by the pope dates back at least to the fourth century. The custom of conferring it on other bishops dates to the sixth century. In 1973, Pope Paul VI restricted the conferral of pallia to metropolitan archbishops only. The

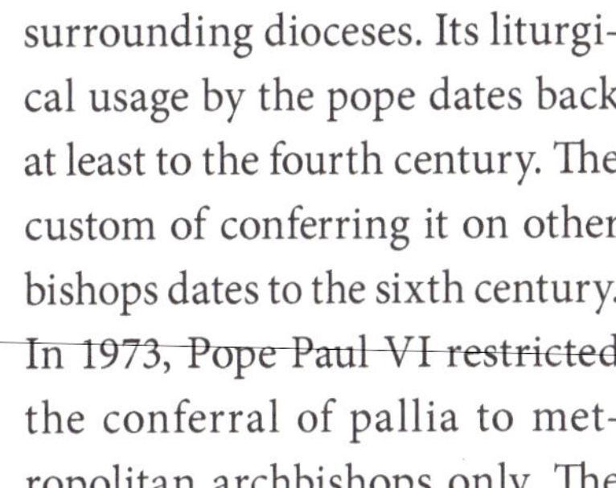

pallium is worn by a metropolitan archbishop over the chasuble during the celebration of the Mass within his ecclesiastical province.

The word "pallium" is derived from the Latin *palla*, meaning "woolen cloak." Today, the pallium is a three-inch-wide white band with a lappet, or tail-like piece of cloth, on the front. An archbishop's pallium is decorated with six black crosses. The pope's pallium has red crosses. Three pins were used to hold the pallium together, but now they are just decorative.

The pallium is woven from lamb's wool by nuns of the Basilica of Santa Cecilia in Trastevere in Rome. The wool is from carefully selected lambs that are donated by the Cistercian monks at the Tre Fontane Abbey in Rome. On their way to the Basilica of Santa Cecilia, these lambs are blessed at the Basilica of Saint Agnes Outside the Walls on the morning of January 21, which is the liturgical memorial of Saint Agnes.

The finished pallia were traditionally blessed by the pope and presented to new archbishops on June 29, the Solemnity of Sts. Peter and Paul; this tradition continues today. New metropolitan archbishops receive their pallia from the papal nuncio (ambassador of the pope) in their respective archdioceses. The pallium symbolizes the unity of the archbishop with the pope.

Faithful Reflections

Perhaps the most important piece of clothing we own is our baptismal gown. Not the one we wore as a small child at our baptism, but the one we wear each day. Our baptismal gown is not an outer garment but rather an inner attitude. The letter to the Galatians states that those who were baptized into Christ have clothed themselves with Christ. (See Galatians 3:27.) The Letter to the Colossians encourages us to "put on then, as God's chosen ones, holy and beloved, heartfelt compassion, kindness, humility, gentleness, and patience, bearing with one another and forgiving one another.... And over all these put on love, that is, the bond of perfection" (Colossians 3:12–14). Though liturgical vesture does symbolize distinct ministries, in the end it is not by our clothing but by our actions that we will be recognized and judged. For, as Jesus said, "This is how all will know that you are my disciples, if you have love for one another" (John 13:35).

Look closely at the vestments at your church. What do you notice? The liturgy is to support and serve the building up of the kingdom of God. All that we express symbolically, including vesture and all the accents and jewelry, is to do the same. You may know the expression "wearing your heart on your sleeve." This is how Christians are to witness at all times.

- ✠ *What type of clothing do you feel most comfortable wearing? Why?*
- ✠ *What events compel you to think about what you are wearing with care? What clothing fully expresses your faith?*
- ✠ *What vesture do you often see at your church, and what does it signify? What don't you see?*

CHAPTER EIGHT

The Symbolic Meaning of Liturgical Gestures

When my grandfather unexpectedly died at home, we opened all the windows immediately, as was customary at the time, so his spirit could leave the house. We also stopped all the clocks. The funeral directors came to the house and turned the living room into a funeral chapel by draping the walls and windows with black curtains. Large candelabras flanked my grandfather's body, laid out in a coffin. The entire house was filled with dark quiet.

On the day of the funeral, pallbearers carried my grandfather's casket to the hearse. We followed the hearse by foot, making our way to the church while the death toll was ringing. After the service, we walked to the cemetery. The procession was led by servers with a cross and candles, followed by priests dressed in cassocks with surplices and black stoles. Passersby stopped for a moment, removed their hats, and bowed their heads. We gathered around an open tomb while my grandfather's coffin was lowered into it, and all of us threw handfuls of dirt on the coffin as we filed by.

Everyone was dressed in black, and the women wore black veils. Our immediate family wore black for six months, and then we were allowed to wear gray and dark blue for the following six months. It was only after marking the one-year anniversary of my grandfather's death that we were allowed to again wear colors.

Much has changed since that time. Today, the custom of wearing black for great lengths of time after the loss of a loved one has completely disappeared. Family members go to the cemetery but rarely wait for the coffin to be lowered into the ground. Some cemeteries advise people to say their last goodbyes in a special chapel on the grounds rather than going to the graveside. In these cases, only after everyone has left is the coffin brought to the burial plot and lowered into the tomb. While well-intended, the disappearance of these rituals and customs deprives us of ways that help us grieve. Such gestures as waking the body at home, walking behind the hearse, throwing soil on the coffin, and wearing distinctive clothing help us express our deep feelings of loss.

Though our society is the poorer for losing many of our rituals, Catholic rituals and liturgies are still packed with gestures that help us celebrate moments of great joy or mark important transitions in our lives. We submerge one another in water, we anoint with oil, we gather around the Easter fire, we wash feet and sometimes kiss them, we break bread and share it with one another, we drink from one cup, we receive ashes at the beginning of Lent, we burn incense, we light candles, we genuflect and kneel and prostrate on the ground, we hug, we touch, and we kiss the *Gospel Book*, the cross, the altar, and sometimes one another. We are the *body* of Christ, and our liturgy celebrates the physicality of the body of Christ. We express who we are as Christians with words, symbols, and gestures while simultaneously impressing on ourselves who we are as Christians.

THOUGH OUR SOCIETY IS THE POORER FOR LOSING MANY OF OUR RITUALS, CATHOLIC RITUALS AND LITURGIES ARE STILL PACKED WITH GESTURES THAT HELP US CELEBRATE MOMENTS OF GREAT JOY OR MARK IMPORTANT TRANSITIONS IN OUR LIVES.

About symbolic postures to be used for the Eucharist, the *GIRM* states, "A common posture, to be observed by all those taking part is a sign of the unity of the members of the Christian community gathered together for the sacred liturgy" (*GIRM* 42). It is important, then, for the whole body to know these liturgical gestures so that we can do them together.

Processions

In many parts of the world, grand outdoor processions are still very popular. They mark Holy Week and the solemnity of Corpus Christi as well as the feasts of local patron saints. Though there is a resurgence of these in the United States, most of us are familiar with more modest practices, such as the entrance procession at the beginning of Mass, the gospel procession, the procession with the gifts, the Communion procession, and the closing procession.

Liturgical processions serve the practical purpose of moving people from one place to another. However, if processions were merely practical, then it would be much more efficient to have the priest and servers walk from the sacristy in a direct line to the sanctuary. Instead, they take a somewhat circuitous route and may add additional people to the procession. The people in the procession often bring with them a liturgical object that will be used in the liturgy, such as the *Gospel Book*. Thus, in addition to being practical, liturgical processions are also—and, more importantly—symbolic. Processions are a symbolic embodiment of our journey from baptism to burial, which does not always take a direct route and is never walked alone.

A couple of times each year, the entire congregation participates in the opening procession. On Palm Sunday of our Lord's Passion, everyone joins the commemorative procession of Jesus' entrance into Jerusalem. During the Easter Vigil, after lighting the Easter candle from the Easter fire, everyone processes into the church, holding candles lit from the Easter candle. Most of the time, however, only a representative group joins in the procession. And yet, even though we may not be able to physically participate, the procession represents each one of us, and all of us participate spiritually.

Some processions—such as a Gospel procession or the procession with the gifts—are highly orchestrated. There are also more informal processions, such as the gathering "procession" that begins when we leave our individual homes to come to church. This procession starts as a series of smaller processions that meet in the church parking lot and culminate in the entrance procession, the formal beginning of the liturgy. At the end of Mass, we see the grand opening procession in reverse as the formal liturgical procession processes out, followed by the assembly, who then split into numerous smaller processions as everyone makes their way home and back to their daily lives.

Processions in churches in the West are highly choreographed and stylized. A typical gospel procession in the West comprises incense, candles, and the ordained minister, who is carrying the *Gospel Book* in a stately walk to the ambo. By contrast, processions in other parts of the world can be very dynamic and have a level of spontaneity. A gospel procession in Cameroon, for instance, has many people involved. They all gather around one person, who carries the *Gospel Book* , which is wrapped in beautiful cloth, on his or her back. The person carrying the *Gospel Book* is bent down, struggling under the weight of the message but moving forward, encouraged by the people around him or her. Once the procession reaches the sanctuary, the priest or deacon takes the *Gospel Book* and raises it high while everyone bursts out in ululation.

Genuflecting

Upon entering a church, we traditionally perform a series of actions. First, we make our way past the baptismal font, where we touch the water, make the sign of the cross, and remind ourselves of our baptismal rights and obligations. Then, we proceed into the nave, the main body of the church, where we genuflect as a sign of reverence toward the Blessed Sacrament, reserved in the tabernacle. If the Blessed Sacrament is reserved in a separate chapel, we make a profound bow toward the altar which, once consecrated, is a permanent symbol of Christ. Both actions are threshold gestures that assist us in making the transition from the profane to the sacred, from the secular world to the sacred realm of the liturgy.

We also genuflect every time we pass before the Blessed Sacrament, whether it is reserved in the tabernacle or exposed in the monstrance. We do this out of reverence for the Real Presence of Christ in the Blessed Sacrament. During the celebration of the liturgy, we genuflect when we enter and leave the sanctuary, if the tabernacle is in the sanctuary. The practice of genuflecting on both knees when the Blessed Sacrament is exposed is no longer customary; a single genuflection is always an appropriate expression of reverence.

The Sign of the Cross

There are several moments in the Mass when we sign ourselves with the sign of the cross. After the opening procession, the celebrant leads us in the sign of the cross. This is our mark. It sets us apart as Christians. The cross is our sign because it is by the cross that we have been saved. The cross is the instrument of our salvation. Every time we gather, we gather "in the name of the Father, the Son and the Holy Spirit," and we make the sign of the cross.

During the Liturgy of the Word, we sign ourselves when the priest announces the gospel by saying, "A reading from the holy Gospel according to...." We respond by saying, "Glory to you, O Lord," while at the same time marking our forehead, lips, and heart with the sign of the cross. This gesture indicates our desire and hope that the word of God we are about to hear may be in our mind, on our lips, and in our heart, so that we may be inspired by the word, willing to testify to the word, and moved to live it as we carry the word in our heart.

At the end of Mass, the celebrant sends us into the world to live as the body of Christ. Before we leave, he calls down God's blessing upon us as he signs us with the sign of our salvation to give us strength for our journey of faith and all we encounter beyond the doors of the liturgy.

Orans

The term "orans" comes from the Latin verb *orare,* which means "to pray." Orans refers to a specific prayer posture in which both hands are extended upward in prayer. The gesture predates Christianity and is currently used in various religions.

The oldest images of Christians depicted in the orans position are in the Roman catacombs, an ancient, complex system of tunnels used to bury early Christians, among others. In hundreds of instances, a woman is portrayed standing, with her hands raised up to heaven in prayer. These women are believed to represent the souls of the deceased, pleading for mercy, whether the deceased be male or female. Early depictions of Mary and the saints also show them in the orans position as they plead for God's mercy in prayer.

The priest at Mass uses the orans gesture when he prays to God on behalf of the people. This includes the opening and closing prayer of the Mass, the prayer over the gifts, the Eucharistic prayer, and the Lord's Prayer.

Many assemblies have developed a custom of extending their hands in the orans position during the Lord's Prayer. This is neither suggested nor forbidden in the rubrics that guide the details of the celebration of the Eucharist, although it can be seen as quite a symbol of unity when all people extend their hands in the same position while praying the same prayer. Some congregations hold hands during the

Lord's Prayer to show this unity. Again, there are no rubrics for or against this. However, the ancient gesture of the orans, practiced for many centuries, seems more appropriate than a newer expression that holds less meaning.

The Washing of the Priest's Hands

Many religions perform ablutions or washings with water as part of their ritual and prayer. This may include a ritual washing of the feet, hands, and face, or even of the whole body. There are two components to the ritual of washing: one is practical, and the other is symbolic. On a purely practical level, washing is intended to simply clean the worshipper's face, hands, feet, or body. The symbolic meaning of washing varies from ritual to ritual and from religion to religion but usually alludes to a spiritual cleansing.

While on retreat in Assisi many years ago, I attended Mass at San Damiano on October 4, the memorial of St. Francis. The Mass was celebrated in the courtyard of the monastery, where St. Clare of Assisi started the women's branch of the Franciscans. To my surprise, the offertory procession included several locals carrying vegetables, fruit, eggs, and even chickens and a lamb. This is probably what happened at the time of St. Francis and quite different from the highly stylized procession with the gifts we know today. The celebrant of the Mass received all these gifts and placed them around the well in the center of the courtyard, which functioned as a temporary altar. When he washed his hands using soap and water, I was reminded that some of the purely spiritual rituals at Mass have very practical origins. Having handled the produce and the animals, washing his hands was well advised.

Today, the procession of the gifts consists mostly of monetary gifts, bread, and wine. Incensing, too, has become more contained and does not require the same type of cleanup as in days past. As a result, the washing of hands is purely symbolic and spiritual, as its meaning has shifted from the cleansing of actual dirt to a spiritual cleansing. The custom of using a disinfectant during the COVID pandemic was a temporary return to the once-practical function.

The washing of the hands by the priest is sometimes referred to in Latin as *lavabo*. This is a reference to the words spoken by the priest while he is washing his hands in the Tridentine Mass: "*Lavabo inter innocentes manus meas, et circumibo altare tuum, Domine,*" or "I will wash my hands in innocence so that I may process around your altar, Lord" (Psalm 26:6). The current version of the Roman Rite prescribes that the priest washes his hands while standing to the side of the altar and quietly saying, "Wash me, O Lord, from my iniquity and cleanse me from my sin." (See Psalm 51).

Though the washing of hands currently is done by only the priest, there was a time when everyone did so. Basilicas built by emperor Constantine after the legalization of Christianity in 313 had a large courtyard, also known as an *exonarthex*. In its center was a large fountain where everyone stopped to wash their hands, feet, and faces in preparation for entering the

church. Monasteries also had designated places where monks stopped to wash their hands on their way to church.

The Washing of the Feet

Several years ago, I decided to celebrate the Sacred Triduum at the motherhouse of a religious community. Having arrived early, I spent some quiet time in the monastery chapel in preparation for the Mass of the Lord's Supper on Holy Thursday. From my chair in the back row, I watched the sisters arrive for the liturgy. Many of them were quite elderly. They used wheelchairs, walkers, or another sister's arm to make their way into the chapel. The priest and I were the only men in the chapel.

At the time of the washing of the feet, the priest washed the feet of twelve of the sisters. This was before Pope Francis lifted the liturgical mandate that only men were to have their feet washed by the celebrant, so it took me by surprise. After he was done washing feet, the celebrant surprised me again by inviting the sisters to wash one another's feet.

One of the sisters caught my attention as she made her way to the front of the chapel. With great difficulty, she knelt before one of the sisters in a wheelchair. Gently, she took the slippers off her sister's gnarled feet. A bowl with water was brought to them. She placed her sister's feet in the water and tenderly washed them. Then she dried them and kissed them. These feet, which had walked in the service of the Church for more than seventy years, were tenderly washed by hands that had served the Church for more than sixty years. It was a very moving manifestation of the power of this important ritual.

The washing of the feet is not a superfluous gesture or a simple reenactment of what Jesus did 2,000 years ago. Rather, it is an efficacious ritual rehearsal of what all of us are called to do every day of our life: serve one another.

On the night of the Last Supper, Jesus instructed his disciples to do two things. According to the synoptic Gospels of St. Matthew, St. Mark, and St. Luke, Jesus told them to break bread and share the cup. According to the Gospel of St. John, Jesus mandated his disciples to wash one another's feet. (See John 13:1–17.) There is evidence that both mandates were followed by early Christians. Several Church Fathers refer to the washing of the feet as being done in imitation of Christ and as a way to "teach one's hands to serve others."

In the fifty-third chapter of his *Rule*, St. Benedict (480–537) writes, "The abbot shall pour water on the hands of the guests, and the abbot with the entire community shall wash their feet." This was a profoundly spiritual act, for in their guests, "Christ himself is honored and received." As late as the twelfth century, St. Bernard (1090–1153) considered the washing of the feet to be a sacrament. In one of his homilies preached on Holy Thursday, he recommended foot-washing as "a daily sacrament for the remission of sins."

Washing the feet of those who were to be baptized was a custom in such places as North Africa, Milan, and Gaul but never in Rome. The Synod of Toledo of 694 required all bishops and priests in a position of authority to wash the feet of those subject to them under pain of excommunication.

The connection between Holy Thursday and the washing of the feet was established in Rome at least by the twelfth century, when the pope washed the feet of twelve sub-deacons after celebrating Mass and the feet of thirteen poor men after his dinner. The 1570 *Missal* of Pope Pius V refers to the washing of feet after the Holy Thursday Mass without being connected to the Mass itself. It was not until 1955, when as part of his sweeping changes to the celebration of Holy Week, Pope Pius XII integrated the washing of the feet into the Mass of the Lord's Supper on Holy Thursday. Ever since, after the homily, the celebrant has washed the feet of twelve men, referencing the twelve apostles, though this number is not specified in the *Missal*. In 2013, Pope Francis broke the custom of washing the feet only of men by washing the feet of women during his Holy Thursday Mass. The *Roman Missal* was updated in 2016 to ratify this change.

The Sign of Peace

There exists a wonderful icon of St. Peter and St. Paul greeting one another with a holy kiss of peace. This icon portrays the original greeting between Christians as a kiss. This type of greeting was common both inside and outside of the liturgy. When this practice became objectionable, a new custom was developed that replaced kissing another person. A new liturgical object, known as a pax table or peace table, was introduced. The priest celebrating Mass would kiss the pax table, which was a type of metal plate, then wipe the plate and give it to someone else, who would do the same and then present it to the next person. The fact that the sign of peace started with the priest emphasized the fact that the peace shared among Christians comes from Christ.

The 1570 *Missal* of Pope Pius V did away with the sign of peace except during High Mass, and then shared only among the clergy. The sign of peace shared by everyone present was reintroduced in the 1969 *Missal* of Pope Paul VI.

Despite the ancient custom, the Church recognizes that kissing strangers is not universally accepted, so other options have been provided, such as hug, a handshake, or a bow. During the sign of peace in the United States, it is common to shake the hand of those we don't know well and to hug or kiss friends or family with whom we are more familiar. In this post-COVID time, many people have taken to waving to one another or making the sign of peace with their hands. Whereas in the past, the sign of peace was exchanged with people in one's immediate vicinity, the post-COVID practice has evolved into greeting more and more people, albeit from a greater distance.

More important than the type of gesture is the understanding that the peace we share with one another has its foundation in Jesus Christ, the source of our lasting peace, the One who grants us peace, and the One who invites us into peace. As Christians who share in that peace, we are to share it with one another. Therefore, before we approach the table of the Lord at Communion, we affirm our unity in the peace of Christ by sharing a sign of peace with one another.

The Commingling

The symbolic gesture of commingling is the moment during Mass when the celebrant breaks a small piece of the host and drops it into the chalice. While he does that, he quietly says, "May this mingling of the Body and Blood of our Lord Jesus Christ bring eternal life to us who receive it." The commingling takes place during the fraction rite after the sign of peace and before receiving holy Communion. The Lamb of God is sung at that time.

The origins of commingling date back to the early Church. As early as the second century, bishops, after celebrating Mass, would send part of the eucharistic bread, known as *fermentum,* or "leaven," to nearby bishops. The bishop who received the *fermentum* added it to the cup and consumed it during the next Mass he celebrated. This is believed to have been done as a sign of unity among the bishops. The pope, too, sent out *fermentum* to the bishops as a sign of unity. The term *fermentum* may have been used because the Eucharist is understood to be the leaven of our Christian life, and we are to be leaven for the world.

As Christianity spread throughout the Roman Empire, particularly outside of the cities

into the countryside, it became necessary for the bishops to send some of their priests into the rural areas. These priests represented the bishop to these communities and celebrated the Eucharist on Sundays. To affirm the unity between the bishop and these communities, deacons brought the *fermentum* or a part of the eucharistic bread that had been consecrated by the bishop to the outlying areas.

Today, this particle of the host no longer comes to us from the bishop, nor from a previous Mass, yet the priest still adds a small piece of the consecrated host to the cup. It is no longer called the *fermentum*, but "commingling," and primarily symbolizes the unity of the Body and Blood of Christ, as well as the unity of our sharing in the Body of Christ at Mass and our hope in the resurrection.

Kneeling

There are many references to kneeling in the Bible. The psalmist invites us to kneel in prayer: "Enter, let us bow down in worship; let us kneel before the LORD who made us" (Psalm 95:6). King Solomon knelt in prayer at the dedication of the temple. (See 2 Chronicles 6:13.) David knelt in prayer three times a day. (See Daniel 6:11.) Jesus knelt while praying. (See Luke 22:41.) And, after addressing them and before leaving, Paul knelt in prayer with the presbyters of Ephesus.

The posture of kneeling reflects and encourages humility, reverence, and adoration. Because of that, kneeling is a great posture for prayer in general and for the celebration of the Eucharist in particular. The *GIRM* states, "In the dioceses of the United States of America, [the faithful] should kneel beginning after the singing or recitation of the Sanctus (Holy, Holy, Holy) until after the Amen of the Eucharistic Prayer, except when prevented on occasion by reasons of health, lack of space, of the large number of people present, or some other good reason.... The faithful kneel after the Agnus Dei unless the diocesan bishop determines otherwise" (*GIRM* 43).

In addition to kneeling during the Eucharistic Prayer, it is also proper to kneel while in the presence of the Blessed Sacrament during exposition at least for some time, out of reverence for the presence of Christ in the Blessed Sacrament. Kneeling during the sacrament of reconciliation as a gesture of humility and repentance is also appropriate. In addition to our common liturgical posture of kneeling, many people find that kneeling during private prayer helps their prayer and deepens their spirituality, especially during a penitential season such as Lent.

Being Silent

Most of us prefer to be bathed in sound rather than allowing the refreshing qualities of silence to wash over us. Sitting alone in silence or allowing silence to be part of time spent with friends is increasingly more uncomfortable.

And, yet, silence is a soothing balm for the soul, something desperately needed given our very complex world and demanding lives.

Silence is not the mere absence of noise or the suspension of speech. Silence is profound stillness. God speaks to us from the eternal silence. As such, silence is an essential component of our liturgical celebrations.

It is in silence that God's word finds its way to our heart. That is why a moment of silence is observed after each reading and at the conclusion of the Liturgy of the Word. Silence invites meditation and allows for adoration. That is why a moment of silence is observed at the time of the elevation of the Body and Blood of Christ during the consecration as well as after the reception of holy Communion. Silence also allows for personal prayer. That is why the celebrant pauses after his invitation to all of us to offer our individual prayers in silence when he says, "Let us pray." The celebrant then gathers all our prayers into a prayer he speaks aloud.

Given our preference for sound over silence, it is not surprising that silence does not come easily. Silence is a discipline that is learned over time. It presumes a willingness to let go of our preoccupation with time. Silence requires that we are present to the moment. Such distractions as the anticipated length of Mass or what comes next need to be overcome.

Experiencing silence during the liturgy also serves as a model for our personal lives and the positive impact it can have on our spiritual health. Short moments of silence experienced at the beginning and at the end of the day offer opportunities to meditate on God's benevolent presence in our lives, for which we give thanks. Silence can also teach us how to listen for God's guidance.

Placing of Ashes

The custom of imposing ashes on Ash Wednesday has biblical and liturgical roots. In all instances, it is a sign of repentance and sorrow. The Book of Esther tells the story of how Mordecai mourned when he learned of the plot to kill all the Jewish people. "When Mordecai learned all that was happening, he tore his garments, put on sackcloth and ashes, and went through the city crying out loudly and bitterly, till he came before the royal gate, which no one clothed in sackcloth might enter. Likewise in each of the provinces, wherever the king's decree and law reached, the Jews went into deep mourning, with fasting, weeping, and lament; most of them lay on sackcloth and ashes" (Esther 4:1–3).

Job used ashes as a sign of repentance: "Therefore I disown what I have said, and repent in dust and ashes" (Job 42:6). Jesus, too, spoke about ashes as a sign of repentance: "Then he began to reproach the towns where most of his mighty deeds had been done, since they had not repented. 'Woe to you, Chorazin! Woe to you, Bethsaida! For if the mighty deeds done in your midst had been done in Tyre and Sidon, they would long ago have repented in sackcloth and ashes'" (Matthew 11:20–21).

The liturgical custom of sprinkling ashes is undoubtedly inspired by the biblical use, and it probably originates in the Order of Penitents, which was created in response to a pressing need. At stake was salvation for those who had gravely sinned after baptism. Venial sins were forgiven through participation in Sunday Eucharist, but grave sins were not. Because the sacrament of reconciliation did not exist yet, and a second baptism for the forgiveness of sins was not an option, the Order of Penitents was established to give people a second chance. Being part of this order was no easy task. First, one had to be admitted to the order by the bishop. At the beginning of Lent, penitents were ceremoniously cast out of the church, made to prostrate, and were covered with ashes. They had to wear certain clothes to be recognizable. They had designated seats in church and were made to leave after the gospel. They often did not work and begged for food. The time of penance sometimes lasted years. When they were ready, they were readmitted to the community, usually on Holy Thursday.

Because it was not possible to be admitted to the Order of Penitents a second time, it eventually gave way to the sacrament of reconciliation, which can and ought to be celebrated regularly. Yet, the custom of imposing ashes was so effective that it was retained on Ash Wednesday as a powerful way to mark the beginning of the penitential season of Lent.

Ash Wednesday was formally established in 601 by Pope Gregory the Great. Because fasting

was not done on Sundays, the addition of the four days before the first Sunday of Lent allowed for a full forty-day period of fasting and penance. The custom of distributing ashes on everyone participating in Ash Wednesday liturgy dates to the eighth to tenth centuries. Ashes were first generously strewn on the crown of the head rather than as a cross on the forehead. The original way of distributing ashes still survives in some places, such as in Rome. The more ancient words used by the minister during the sprinkling of ashes are, "Remember that you are dust, and to dust you shall return." (See Genesis 3:19.) These are the words God spoke when expelling Adam and Eve from paradise, thus subjecting them to death. An alternative was adapted after the Second Vatican Council: "Repent and believe in the gospel."

The ashes used in the liturgy of Ash Wednesday come from the palms that were blessed during the previous year's celebration of Palm Sunday of Our Lord's Passion.

Faithful Reflections

Guests at a Catholic liturgy are sometimes amazed by the many postures that are a part of our prayer. Our ritual invites us to be present not only with our minds but also with our bodies as we process, genuflect, kneel, sit, stand, bow, and prostrate. More amazing is that at times we might do these gestures automatically, without understanding what they mean or knowing why we do them. When we slow down, we might realize we don't think about them much at all. Take some time to meditate on one or two of these gestures the next time you participate in Mass. Think about how your body feels as you kneel and pray or when you bow to the altar as if Christ were standing there in front of you—that is, in fact, what we are doing. Sometimes, we don't know what to say when we come to prayer, yet one gesture can say it all. What would it be like to pray without words and let our bodies do the talking?

- *What actions in your life do you do without thinking? What do you do by routine?*
- *Make a point to really think about what you are doing when you sign yourself with the sign of the cross at the beginning of Mass. What would it be like to bless a family member or friend with the sign of the cross?*
- *How do you experience liturgical gestures outside of Mass? What is the difference between standing in line at Communion and standing in line at the grocery store? What are other liturgical gestures that might offer an opportunity for reflection beyond the church doors?*

CHAPTER NINE

The Symbolic Meaning of Liturgical Décor

Liturgical décor plays a vital role in the celebration of the liturgy by engaging the senses and contributing to the overall liturgical experience for the congregation. The power of the senses and their role in the liturgy cannot be overestimated, as they can transport us into another world, beyond our knowing. This became exceedingly clear during a trip to Iceland to witness the midnight sun.

I had never been to Iceland, and I was looking forward not only to experiencing the midnight sun but also to finding out more about the mythic gnomes, elves, giants, and "hidden people" for which Iceland is known. From the moment we landed, I was enchanted. Iceland is 99 percent volcanic desert, so arriving there is almost like landing on the moon, or so I imagined.

THROUGHOUT THE COURSE OF THE LITURGICAL YEAR, THE DÉCOR CHANGES TO SUPPORT AND ENHANCE THE MEANING OF THE SEASONS AND FEASTS.

As I was marveling at the landscape on our way to Reykjavik, the capital of Iceland, the cab driver stopped unexpectedly and told us to get out and have a look at the geysers and shacks in the distance. Abandoning our suitcases in the cab, my traveling companion and I hiked through a volcanic landscape dotted by geysers to a vast collection of shacks, where we discovered fish heads hanging on strings, drying in the wind and the sun. The combination of the smell of sulfur produced by the geyser and the smell of drying fish created an olfactory experience that is not easily forgotten.

We continued to Reykjavik and, after dinner, set out for a walk through the city. As anticipated, the sun did not set, but only dipped to the horizon before rising again. This movement created very elongated shadows in the city that, accompanied by fog, set the stage for the folklore of elves and giants to come to life.

While admiring the Lutheran cathedral that is intriguingly shaped like a geyser, I realized we were surrounded by eerily lifelike statues of gnomes and elves rising from low wafts of fog. It was all a bit unsettling. Then, suddenly, an elderly woman appeared out of nowhere, as if she were one of the sculptures come to life. She asked if we had heard that the night belongs to the "hidden people." We told her we had not. As she swung her scarf around my neck, pulling me in, she hissed that we would die before the rising of the sun. In complete and absolute fear, I pushed her away and ran toward the safety of my locked hotel room. Although I knew perfectly well that giants and gnomes do not exist, the sensory experiences led me to imagine that we would be killed by gnomes and would not leave the island alive.

Despite any logic, our senses picked up explicit and implicit messages that amplified the prophetic words of the old woman. This is how liturgical décor engages the senses—through sight and sound and smell to better communicate its message of faith.

How often have I heard people say, "It smells like Christmas," when they enter a church filled with evergreens? Or, "It smells like Easter," when they approach a baptismal font festooned with Easter lilies? Throughout the course of the liturgical year, the décor changes to support and enhance the meaning of the seasons and feasts. Some seasons are marked by more modest décor, while others are more exuberant and filled with abundant symbols as we remember the fullness of Christ's life, death, and resurrection.

Seasonal Symbols for the Incarnation Cycle

The Incarnation season includes the liturgical seasons of Advent and Christmas. The word "Advent" originates from the Latin phrase *Adventus Domini*, meaning "the arrival of the Lord." It refers to Jesus' appearance on earth over 2,000 years ago, his presence with us today, and especially his coming at the end of time. Thus, the season of Advent is filled with anticipation for the commemoration of the birth of Jesus. And it is a time of preparation for his final manifestation, the Second Coming. Christmas celebrates the fullness of these realities: Jesus' presence among us yesterday, today, and tomorrow.

The Advent Wreath

The origin of the Advent wreath is unclear. There is evidence of a pre-Christian custom of decorating a wheel with candles while prayers were offered for the wheel of the earth to be turned so that light and warmth would return. Christians then adopted this ritual in the Middle Ages and began to use it in domestic settings. By the year 1500, however, more formal practices surrounding the Advent wreath had developed, with the totality of the wreath symbolizing new and eternal life gained through the mystery of the life, death, and resurrection of Jesus Christ.

The symbols of light and life of the Advent wreath apply very easily to the Christian belief that Christ is both the light that dispels darkness and the life of the world. The wreath itself, a circle with neither beginning nor end, signifies eternal life. The evergreens, too, represent eternal life because, unlike deciduous trees, they stay green in winter. In addition to evergreens, people might add holly, implying immortality; cedar, expressing strength and healing; laurel, touting victory over suffering; and pinecones and nuts, extolling life and resurrection.

The four candles that were added to the wreath over time represent the four weeks of Advent. According to some traditions, these candles are purple, connecting them to the color of the Advent season. Sometimes, the color of the candle for the third Sunday of Advent is rose, like the vestments for that day. This color celebrates the fact that we have reached the midpoint of Advent. The Latin name for this day is, not surprisingly, Gaudete Sunday. *Gaudete* means "rejoice" and is the first word of the Latin Introit for Mass for this day.

Though it started as a domestic custom, the Advent wreath is the central symbol of the Advent season in most churches. The candles are often purple and rose, but they may also be white. The liturgy may include a blessing of the wreath and ceremonial candle lighting on the first Sunday of Advent. This blessing, however, is not found in the *Roman Missal* but rather in the *Catholic Book of Blessings*.

The long tradition of Advent wreaths in the homes of Christians is a laudable custom. Advent wreaths can be easily constructed. The

candle for each week can be lit and blessed as part of a prayer before a meal on the Saturdays or Sundays of Advent. The prayers for these blessings can be found in the *Catholic Book of Blessings*.

The Christmas Tree

The earliest reports of decorated trees date back to ancient Roman times, when small trees were decorated with pieces of polished metal during the winter festival of Saturnalia, honoring Saturn, the god of agriculture. During the Middle Ages, Adam and Eve were commemorated with mystical plays on Christmas Eve, and an evergreen was decorated with apples to symbolize the tree of paradise. Some people believe that Martin Luther was the first to introduce a tree decorated with candles into the home after he was inspired by the star-filled sky he encountered during a walk through the woods on a clear Christmas night.

By the nineteenth century, the custom of decorating trees in people's homes had become very popular in the Western Hemisphere. It was an image of a young Queen Victoria and her family gathered around a Christmas tree, published in the *Illustrated London News* in 1848, that popularized the tradition. Today, more than thirty-five million Christmas trees are sold in the United States each year for use in private homes, public places, and as part of the Christmas décor in our churches.

Whether it is placed outside or inside the church, a Christmas tree is a wonderful symbol of the tree of life, the tree of paradise. It brings joy to people's hearts as they indulge in feelings of nostalgia from childhood memories, and it invites people to look toward the future, when the promise of eternal life will be fulfilled. Christmas trees not only offer a visual enhancement to the liturgical décor but also add a scent that immediately greets all who come to worship, signaling that Christmas has arrived. The church looks like Christmas and smells like Christmas.

The Crib, Crèche, or Manger

The nativity scene is known by several different names in English. "Crèche" is from an Old French word that is derived from the Old High German *Krippa*, meaning "crib." Some people refer to the nativity scene simply as "the crib." The word "manger," from the Old English *mangeour*, is derived from the Old French *maingeure* ("to eat"), which in turn is derived from the Latin *manducare* ("to chew"). So, while both words (crèche and manger) relate to the place where Jesus was laid, one is a baby's crib, and the other a feeding trough. The latter, of course, is more in line with the Scriptures: "She gave birth to her firstborn son. She wrapped him in swaddling clothes and laid him in a manger, because there was no room for them in the inn" (Luke 2:7).

One of the oldest examples of a crèche is carved into the lid of a sarcophagus dating back to the end of the fourth or beginning of the fifth century. In the depiction, Jesus is wrapped in swaddling clothes and lying in a manger. Joseph and Mary are not represented. On either side of Jesus is an ox and a donkey. These illustrate Isaiah's prophecy: "An ox knows its owner, and an ass, its master's manger" (Isaiah 1:3).

It was not until St. Francis and the Franciscan Order popularized the nativity that a worldwide interest was sparked—first in Italy, then throughout Europe and across the globe. Anxious to return the focus of Christmas festivities to Jesus, St. Francis in 1223 created a nativity with live animals in a cave in Greccio near Assisi. It is believed that he modeled this nativity after one he saw in Bethlehem.

According to St. Francis' biographer, Thomas of Celano, when the people of Greccio learned about this nativity, they joined St. Francis, carrying torches and candles. One of the friars began celebrating Mass. Thomas of Celano wrote that St. Francis "stood before the manger...overcome with love and filled with a wonderful happiness." In this early suffering of the Baby Jesus lying in a manger, St. Francis saw a foreshadowing of the hardships Jesus was to suffer as an adult.

After the death of Francis, crib-making became widespread throughout Europe and eventually throughout the world. Today, nativities are displayed in almost every church at Christmas, as well as in family homes. They come in many different materials, shapes, forms, and colors, representative of the different people who created them.

Epiphany Blessing of Homes

Catholics have a longstanding tradition of blessing places, tools, animals, and one another. A popular Christmas blessing is the blessing of homes on the Solemnity of the Epiphany.

Following Epiphany Mass, an inscription is traditionally written in chalk on the lintel above the main entrance door of people's homes. For the year 2026, the inscription would read: 20 + C + M + B + 26. The numbers on either side of the three letters indicate the year, in this case, 2026. The letters are the first letters of the names of the three Magi: Caspar, Melchior, and Balthasar. They also are the first letters of the Latin phrase *Christus Mansionem Benedicat*, or "May Christ bless this home."

While the inscription is being made, the following prayer is said: "Bless, O Lord God Almighty, this home, that in it there may be health, purity, the strength of victory, humility, goodness and mercy, the fulfillment of your law, and thanksgiving to God the Father and to the Son and to the Holy Spirit." After that, the family walks about the home, sprinkling every room with holy water.

Seasonal Symbols f or the Paschal Cycle

The paschal cycle of Lent and Easter lasts ninety days and celebrates the core of our Christian faith: the mystery of the life, death, and resurrection of Jesus Christ. The three-day-long celebration of the Easter Triduum forms the center of the paschal cycle. This Christian Passover commences at sunset on Holy Thursday and concludes at sunset on Easter Sunday. The Easter Triduum is preceded by a forty-day Lenten period of preparation that runs from Ash Wednesday to Holy Thursday, exclusive of Sundays. The Easter season starts with the octave of Easter, or the eight days of Easter. Each one of these days has the highest liturgical status of solemnity, which means that the Mass is celebrated to the fullest with the Gloria and the Creed. The octave ends on the second Sunday of Easter, also known as Divine Mercy Sunday. The Easter season then continues until Pentecost Sunday, the fiftieth and last day of the Easter season. Décor for the paschal season progresses from Ash Wednesday through Lent and into the Easter season to culminate in the Solemnity of Pentecost.

Lenten Simplicity

The décor for Lent is marked by a sparseness that reflects the penitential character of the season. Therefore, Lenten décor relies more on taking away rather than on adding to the visual environment. Lenten décor is characterized by visual absence rather than visual excess and echoes the seasonal call to abstinence, to

clear our lives of clutter, and to return to the essentials of our faith.

The liturgical color for Lent is purple, except on the fourth Sunday of Lent, when the color is rose. The fourth Sunday of Lent is also known as Laetare Sunday. *Laetare*, or "rejoice," is the first word of the Introit for this day.

Veiling of Crucifixes and Statues

Before the Second Vatican Council, it was customary to veil crucifixes and statues beginning on the fourth Sunday of Lent. During the Celebration of the Lord's Passion, the crucifix that was to be used for veneration was gradually unveiled. After the service, any other crucifixes in the church were also unveiled. Statues were unveiled at the beginning of the Easter Vigil.

The 1969 *Missal* of Saint Paul VI, following the revision of the liturgy after the Second Vatican Council, left the decision to continue this practice to the different bishops' conferences. The United States Conference of Catholic Bishops never voted on this, so at first it was not allowed in the United States. The third edition of *The Roman Missal*, from 2002, specifies that "the practice of covering crosses and images in the Church from the fifth Sunday of Lent is permitted, according to the judgment of the Conferences of Bishops. Crosses remain veiled until the end of the Celebration of the Lord's Passion on Good Friday; images remain veiled until the beginning of the Easter Vigil." The US Conference of Catholic Bishops reviewed the matter, and this time voted to allow the covering of crucifixes and images as described in the *Roman Missal*. However, the covering is allowed yet not required.

The Church has a long tradition of fasting from images and colors during Lent. Medieval paintings on high altars often had back panels

that could be closed during Lent. The inside painting was always very colorful, while the outside panels were painted in gray tones. During penitential seasons, the panels were closed so people would fast from colors yet be encouraged in their Lenten disciplines by the saints and saintly motives painted on the outside panels. Although we fast from colors during penitential seasons, we do not fast from all that the saints have to teach us. On the contrary, we are to focus on the lives of the saints so they may inspire us to become better Christians. The same holds for the cross. Seeing and meditating on the crucified Christ undoubtedly enhances our devotion more so than gazing upon a cloth covering it.

Fonts and Founts

Some churches maintain a custom of emptying baptismal fonts and holy water containers during Lent or even go so far as to fill them with desert metaphors, such as sand and cacti. Although this sort of décor is well-intentioned, it does not raise up the primary focus of the season, which is those preparing for baptism at the Easter Vigil. Nor is it clear how this practice engenders greater commitment on the part of those who are preparing to renew their baptismal vows.

There is, however, an ancient custom of emptying the baptismal font after the Mass of the Lord's Supper on Holy Thursday and leaving it empty on Good Friday. This emptiness emphasizes the anticipation for the new baptismal water that will be blessed during the Easter Vigil.

Décor for the Easter Triduum

The décor for celebrating the liturgies of the Triduum is comprised of the symbols that are used for the liturgies themselves. There is little need to add additional décor, because the liturgy itself provides such rich imagery with its symbols for each of the days.

On Holy Thursday, we wash feet, we process with the gifts for the poor, we carry the Blessed Sacrament, and we strip the altar. On Good Friday, the tabernacle is empty, and we kiss the wood of the cross. On Holy Saturday, we gather around the Easter fire, we light the paschal candle and our individual tapers, and then we process into a darkened church to bless water, dunk the Easter candle into its water, immerse the elect in the font, and, while they are still dripping with the water of new life, anoint them with sacred chrism. Then, they dress in white to re-enter the church and join the offertory procession as gifts from and to our community. Given the number and complexity of the symbols and images that are used during the Triduum, additional décor would detract, rather than enhance, the liturgy during these days.

Décor for Easter

The liturgical color for Easter is white, and it may be enhanced with silver and gold. Altar

paraments and banners may be added to enhance the festive character of the season. After we have fasted from plants and flowers during Lent, it is important to festoon the church with living plants.

Easter lilies have come to symbolize the resurrection both by sight and scent. If they are used, it is extremely important to keep them alive. The Easter season lasts fifty days, and the liturgical décor should reflect that. After the Easter lilies stop blooming, spring flowers can continue this visual expression of new life throughout the Easter season. Silk or even dried flowers are not a good alternative for living flowers during the season when we celebrate new life.

Décor for Pentecost

The decorative strength of the feast of Pentecost lies in its color. Because this day celebrates the descent of the Holy Spirit upon the apostles in the form of flames, the Church chose red as the color of the day. Most church buildings look great when decked out in red. In addition to red vestments, red paraments or ornamental hangings, such as a cover for the ambo and an *antependium,* or hanging for the altar, may be used. Red processional banners can also enhance the processions and celebration, as do any red flowers.

Parishioners can also be invited to wear red that day, since they are the Church at worship and therefore equally deserving of adornment. It is a beautiful and moving sight to see both the church building and the Church dressed in red.

Faithful Reflections

Liturgical décor underscores and supports the visual experience of liturgy and lends itself to creativity. Are there ways in which this can be carried over into our homes? The colors of the liturgical year offer the opportunity to expand décor and seasonality into our homes, offices, wardrobes, and even food. Preparing for each liturgical season can become part of your prayer as an individual, couple, or family as you meditate reflectively while preparing a seasonal meal, decorating your home, and praying each day during the Incarnation and paschal seasons.

- ✠ *What sights and smells of your church touch your soul the most?*
- ✠ *What are the strongest symbols that are part of the liturgical décor in your parish? What makes them meaningful for you?*
- ✠ *What can you do to make each of these seasons more meaningful for you and your family?*

CHAPTER TEN

The Symbolic Meaning of Acronyms, Monograms, and Images

We are surrounded by images every day. They range from bumper stickers on cars to billboards lining the highway to neon signs in windows to sayings and pictures on clothing and jewelry to logos on almost every product in the grocery store. Many of these are secular images, but quite a few are religious. Christian imagery can be rather obvious, such as a cross or depictions of Mary and certain saints. Other Christian imagery is more complex, such as symbols of a pelican or a fish. This very fish symbol is borrowed by evolutionists, who reverse its direction and give it tiny legs. And some imagery is nearly incomprehensible, such as acronyms based on a Greek or Latin phrase.

Our shared competence in interpreting some of these Christian images is quite challenged these days. Beloved saints who used to be very familiar to the community are no longer as easily recognized. And even recognizable saints may carry unfamiliar objects. Most of us can identify St. Joseph or the Sacred Heart of Jesus. However, we may not know why St. Joseph holds a lily or where the image of the Sacred Heart originated. Other images are even more confusing, such as a man carrying a baby on his shoulders, as is the case with St. Christopher, or a woman holding what looks like eyeballs on a platter, as is the case with St. Lucy.

To broaden our understanding and appreciation of Christian imagery, it is helpful to learn about some details to unlock the secrets that are part of many images found in our churches.

Sacred Monograms and Acronyms

Monograms and acronyms are both created by using the initial letters of words. They differ from one another in that the letters of a monogram are superimposed or interwoven to make a design or a motif, and acronyms are typically pronounced as words. At first, Christian monograms were used to discreetly indicate that a residence was owned by a Christian family or that a tomb contained the remains of a Christian. This discretion was especially important during times of persecution.

Today, monograms and acronyms are ubiquitous in our cathedrals, churches, and chapels. They are carved into altars and pulpits, painted on icons and ceilings, and embroidered on vestments, to name but a few. Yet, although monograms and acronyms are more numerous than before, today's Christians are not as familiar with their meaning. Knowing what they represent helps us better understand the art and architecture in our churches and may enhance our prayer life.

TODAY, MONOGRAMS AND ACRONYMS ARE UBIQUITOUS IN OUR CATHEDRALS, CHURCHES, AND CHAPELS. THEY ARE CARVED INTO ALTARS AND PULPITS, PAINTED ON ICONS AND CEILINGS, AND EMBROIDERED ON VESTMENTS, TO NAME BUT A FEW.

Several monograms focus on Christ and consist of a combination of letters that refer to the name of Jesus Christ. These are also known as Christograms. The most common and most ancient of all Christograms is the combination of the Greek capital letters Chi, **X**, and Rho, **P**. These are often superimposed, with the **X** positioned just below the **P**. They are the first two letters of the Greek name for Christ, ΧΡΙΣΤΟΣ.

Another Christogram consists of three

Greek capital letters—Iota, **I**; Eta, **H**; and Sigma, **S**, which together form **IHS**. These are the first two and the last or the first three letters of the Greek name of Jesus, ΙΗΣΟΥΣ, which have been transliterated using the Latin alphabet. Another form of this monogram used during the Middle Ages was **IHC**. In this case, the letter Sigma, the last letter of the Greek name of Jesus, is transliterated into a **C** rather than an **S**. Another form is when the **I** is replaced with a **J**. Both I and J as well as C and S were used interchangeably in the Latin alphabet until around the eighteenth century. In keeping with this pattern of transliteration, you might see **IHS**, **IHC**, **JHS**, or **JHC**. All four versions of this Christogram refer to Jesus.

A third Christogram is **ICXC**. This Christogram includes the first and last transliterated letters of the Greek versions of Jesus (**IC**) and Christ (**XC**): ΙΗΣΟΥΣ ΧΡΙΣΤΟΣ. Icons of Jesus often contain these letters, but they are split on either side of the icon, with IC for Jesus on the left and XC for Christ on the right. An expanded version of this Christogram is ICXC NIKA, which is the abbreviation and transliteration of ΙΗΣΟΥΣ ΧΡΙΣΤΟΣ ΝΙΚΑ, or Jesus Christ Victor.

Another combination of letters is **ΑΩ**, the Greek letters alpha and omega. These are the first and last letters of the Greek alphabet and refer to Christ as expressed in the Book of Revelation: "'I am the Alpha and the Omega,' says the Lord God, 'the one who is and who was and who is to come, the almighty'" (Revelation 1:8). These words have been ascribed to Jesus Christ. Thus, the letters ΑΩ are a reference to him.

A popular acronym related to Jesus is **INRI**. Though this is not the custom in English, INRI is pronounced as a word in other languages. Most crucifixes have INRI carved into wood or stone above the head of Jesus or written on a small plaque nailed to the cross. This acronym stands for the Latin *Iesus Christus, Rex Iudeorum,* or, in English, "Jesus Christ, King of the Jews." The text comes from the Gospel of John: "Pilate also had an inscription written and put on the cross. It read, 'Jesus the Nazorean, the King of the Jews.' Now many of the Jews read this inscription, because the place where Jesus was crucified was near the city; and it was written in Hebrew, Latin, and Greek" (John 19:19–20).

It is believed that when St. Helena, the mother of Emperor Constantine, traveled to the Holy Land in 325, she recovered parts of the cross on which Jesus was crucified. In addition, she also found the shroud in which the body of Jesus had been wrapped and the tablet, with this inscription, which had been placed on the cross by order of Pontius Pilate. The tablet is known as the *Titulus Crucis.* It was brought to Rome by Pope Gregory the Great at the end of the fifth century and has been preserved in the church of Santa Croce (Holy Cross) in Rome since 1124.

In addition to the Christ-centered monograms, there are monograms that are centered on Mary, the Mother of God. An immensely popular version is the combination of the letters **A** and **M,** either next to one another or laid over each other. There are diverse ways to interpret this acronym. The most theological interpretation is that these are the first letters of the Latin *Auspice Maria*, which means "under the protection of Mary." A more popular interpretation is that they are the first letters of the first two words spoken by the Archangel Gabriel in greeting Mary at the time of the annunciation. These first words were *Ave Maria*, meaning "hail Mary." They are also the first words of the popular prayer to Mary, known by that same name, Hail Mary.

Another monogram for Mary is frequently found on Marian icons. It comprises the Greek capital letters Mu, M; Rho, P; Theta, Θ; and Upsilon, Y (MP Θ Y), which are the first and last letters of ΜΗΤΗΡ ΘΕΟΥ (*Mētēr Theou*), meaning "Mother of God."

All these letter combinations, be they monograms or acronyms, are constant invitations to prayer, even if they are short prayers, such as the Hail Mary. Every time we see **INRI,** it is a reminder of the sacrifice of Christ. Every time we see **AΩ,** it is a reminder of who Christ really is: the beginning and the end of all that is. When we see **AM,** it is a reminder of the role Mary played in the mystery of our salvation as the Mother of Christ. In all three instances, the monograms and acronyms call us to prayer.

Sacred Images

Our churches and other sacred places, like the catacombs, contain sacred images that, like acronyms and monograms, do not always make sense at first glance. What is the meaning of a pelican on the doors of a tabernacle? Why is a winged ox and a winged lion carved into the pulpit? Why are fish used as a decorative element in the baptismal font? These are said to be Christian, but where do they come from, and what do they really mean?

The Fish

The image of a fish is an ancient Christian symbol. Like monograms and acronyms, the fish was introduced as a "secret code" image to allude to Christianity. The image of a fish was used because the Greek word for fish, ἰχθύς (*ichthys*) is an acronym that refers to Jesus. The letters that form ἰχθύς (*ichthys*) are the first letters of Ἰησοῦς Χριστός, Θεοῦ Υἱός, Σωτήρ (***Iesos Christos Huios Theou, Soter***), meaning "Jesus Christ Son of God, Savior."

As with so many symbols, once they were

created, theologians and other inquiring minds attached additional meaning to them. In this case, an obvious connection may be found in the baptismal theology of Tertullian, who referred to Christ as the big fish and all Christians as little fish. This expressive statement led to decorative motifs comprising small fish and one large fish being used in baptismal architecture.

Tertullian's writing and other theological interpretations, such as linking the fish to the miraculous multiplication of the loaves and fishes, added to the richness of the symbol. The Christian fish symbol has become so well-known that Darwinists, who study evolution, have adopted it as their own, though with some changes that challenge the Christian-held theology of creationism. While the Christian fish is oriented to the left, the Darwinist's fish symbol is turned to the right, has little feet added, and sometimes has *Darwin* written inside the outline of the fish.

The Pelican

A popular medieval symbol for Christ is the mother pelican surrounded by her chicks. In most of these images, the mother pelican is shown to be pecking at her chest and allowing her chicks to feed on her blood. Pelicans feed their chicks by regurgitating the fish they ate, which is rather bloody. This led people in the Middle Ages to believe that pelicans fed their chicks with their own blood to the detriment of their own lives. The Christian connection is rather clear: the mother pelican gave her life to save her chicks like Jesus gave his life in order that we might live. However, for those who do not know the story of the pelican, the symbolic meaning of this image is lost, and it becomes merely an image of a pelican.

The pelican image is most often seen on altars, tabernacles, ceilings of eucharistic chapels, vestments, and altar hangings. This image is also present in the hymn *Adoro te Devote,* composed by St. Thomas Aquinas for the feast of Corpus Christi, the Body and Blood of Christ. The second-to-last verse can be translated to "Lord Jesus, Pelican of Mercy, with your precious blood, cleanse me from my sins." For those who are unfamiliar with the symbol of the pelican, this verse might seem strange. And yet, this is such a beautiful link between sacrament and nature.

The Tetramorph

The word "tetramorph" comes from the Greek words *tetra,* meaning "four," and *morph,* meaning "shape." "Tetramorph" thus refers to a combination of four different shapes that together make a whole. In Christianity, this term refers to the symbolic representation of the four evangelists, Mathew, Mark, Luke, and John, who wrote the four accounts we have of the life of Jesus. Each one of the evangelists was identified with one of the four living creatures described in the Book of Ezekiel and the Book of Revelation.

"As I watched, a great stormwind came from the North, a large cloud with flashing fire, a bright glow all around it, and something like polished metal gleamed at the center of the fire. From within it, figures in the likeness of four living creatures appeared. This is what they looked like: They were in human form, but each had four faces and four wings, and their legs were straight, the soles of their feet like the hooves of a bull, gleaming like polished brass. Human hands were under their wings, and the wings of one touched those of another. Their faces and their wings looked out on all their four sides; they did not turn when they moved, but each went straight ahead. Their faces were like this: each of the four had a human face, and on the right the face of a lion, and on the left, the face of an ox, and each had the face of an eagle" (Ezekiel 1:4–10).

"In front of the throne was something that resembled a sea of glass like crystal. In the center and around the throne, there were four living creatures covered with eyes in front and in back. The first creature resembled a lion, the second was like a calf, the third had a face like that of a human being, and the fourth looked like an eagle in flight" (Revelation 4:6–7).

Based on these texts, artists have depicted the four evangelists as these four living creatures, often surrounding the heavenly throne on which Christ is seated. Matthew is represented by the winged man because Matthew's Gospel emphasizes the humanity of Jesus, as illustrated by his focus on Jesus' genealogy and earthly life. The symbolic representation of Mark is the lion because Mark's Gospel begins

with John the Baptist's powerful voice roaring in the wilderness. Luke is associated with the ox, a sacrificial animal, because Luke's Gospel emphasizes the sacrifice of Jesus. And John is seen as the eagle because of the soaring theology of John's Gospel, emphasizing the Divine nature of Christ, the *Logos* (Word) of God.

A popular place for the Tetramorph is on the ambo, or the place from where the gospel is proclaimed. Sometimes, the *Gospel Book* itself is decorated with a Tetramorph. In both instances, the connection between the gospel and the gospel writers is obvious, provided the beholder has the symbolic knowledge of the Tetramorph. Without this knowledge, the cover of the *Gospel Book* may appear unusual.

The Tetramorph is also featured on baptismal fonts, as it represents the life, death, and resurrection of Jesus—into which we are baptized—as narrated by the evangelists. And it has been used on altars because in the Eucharist, we celebrate the life, death, and resurrection of Jesus as narrated in the gospels.

Early Christian Imagery

At the Basilica of Santa Maria in Trastevere in Rome, there is a statue of the Sacred Heart. It has no great artistic value. It is simple plaster, probably bought in one of the many religious-goods stores in Rome. What is striking about this statue is that it is practically covered in handwritten notes. These notes were placed there by people entrusting their needs and concerns to the Sacred Heart. This act of devotional piety occasioned by representations of Jesus, Mary, and the saints takes place in churches throughout the world. It is as if these images provide a portal to the divine, and whomever an image represents becomes the mediator between the person in need and God.

We are so accustomed to being surrounded by religious imagery that inspires our faith, supports our liturgies, and nurtures our devotions. However, this comfort with religious imagery has not been part of our tradition from the beginning. As a matter of fact, early Christians displayed a general timidity toward imagery. On the one hand, Christianity was born out of Judaism, which was strictly aniconic, meaning that Judaism prohibited all representations of the natural and supernatural world out of fear that this might lead to idolatry. On the other hand, early Christians were persecuted during the first three centuries. As a result, they resorted to simple representations of their faith by using such symbols as a fish, a loaf of bread, an anchor, and, later, a shepherd.

By the beginning of the fourth century, Christians were given freedom of expression after Emperor Constantine legalized Christianity throughout the Roman Empire. This allowed Christian art and architecture to flourish, though the fear of idolatry and the lingering memory of Judaism's prohibition of imagery caused continued hesitation and even resulted in the occasional full-fledged period of iconoclasm, when all images were destroyed. It was not until the Second Council of Nicaea (878) that matters were settled once and for all. After tumultuous debates, this council not only denounced iconoclasm but also called for depictions of Christ, Mary, and the saints with the admonition that when one honors an image, one really honors the one represented by the image.

Christian Imagery in the East and West

Over the centuries, the Church in the East and the Church in the West have taken somewhat different paths when it comes to the way in which Jesus, Mary, and the saints are depicted. The East opted for icons, whereas the West embraced a more realistic approach.

An icon is a sacred image of a holy figure, such as Jesus, Mary, angels, or saints. The icon is typically painted on wood, following a prototype or traditional representation that has been handed down from generation to generation. Traditional icons are stylized. They appear somewhat unnatural, elongated, and, at times, even awkward. They are two-dimensional, without any attempt at perspective.

This very specific approach is because icons intend to depict the spiritual essence or heavenly presence of the holy figure portrayed rather than the natural form of their earthly body. Icons emphasize theological truths and rely on symbolic representation.

Icons are venerated and have been used for centuries as a devotional aid in the Eastern Church and more recently in the Church in the West as well. The visible representation of the saints is believed to evoke their invisible presence among us. This in turn makes communion possible between the members of the body of Christ on earth and the glorified members of the body of Christ in heaven.

Typical religious imagery in the West differs greatly from icons, especially since the Renaissance. The western approach, on the one hand, is more realistic. Whereas icons are stylized representations, western artists portrayed saints as they might have appeared in life rather than evoking the heavenly realm. Western imagery plays on believers' curiosity regarding the details of the earthly lives of individual saints.

On the other hand, whereas icons were painted following a prototype that was handed down from iconographer to iconographer and is believed to be divinely inspired, western artists indulged in a more individual interpretation. As a result, one and the same saint can be represented in many different ways, depending on when and where the artist lived. Flemish Renaissance Madonnas, for instance, look like Flemish aristocratic women. In Italy, during the baroque times, the Blessed Mother was depicted as an Italian matron seated in a typical Italian landscape or home. The purpose of western depictions of the saints to an extent is devotional, but it is also educational, inspirational, and even aesthetic.

Popular Images of Jesus

Christ Pantocrator

Christ Pantocrator is one of the oldest and most important depictions of Christ. In ancient churches, it can be found in the most prominent locations, such as in the apse. It represents Christ as a benevolent, though also stern and all-powerful, judge of humanity. The Greek word *Pantocrator* means "the All-Powerful" or "Ruler of All."

In these representations, it is typical for Christ's body to be depicted frontally and at half-length. He is clothed in a *chiton*, or inner robe, and a *himation*, or outer cloak. In his left hand, he holds a book or a scroll; because of this, the depiction is sometimes referred to as Christ the Teacher.

The book is most often closed, but sometimes it is opened to John 8:12: "I am the light of the world. Whoever follows me will not walk in darkness, but will have the light of life." He offers a blessing with his right hand: the thumb and ring finger touch, symbolizing the two natures—divine and human—of Christ, while the remaining three fingers point outward, referring to the three persons of the Holy Trinity.

Jesus is identified by his cruciform halo, which often has the three Greek letters omicron, ὁ; omega, ὢ; and nu, ν—meaning ὁ ὢν or "He Who Is." This is a reference to the revelation of the name of God to Moses in the burning bush. The Greek capital letters IC are often written on Jesus' right side, while the Greek capital letters XC are written to his left. As previously mentioned, these letters form a monogram composed of the first and last letters of Jesus Christ in Greek: ΙΗΣΟΥΣ ΧΡΙΣΤΟΣ. The last letter of each word, sigma (Σ), is rendered in "C" form.

Christ in Majesty

On the last Sunday of the liturgical year, we celebrate the solemnity of Christ the King. This is a relatively new feast, as it was established by Pope Pius XI in 1925 as an antidote to the growing popularity of nationalist and secularist movements following World War I. With this feast, the Pope hoped to bring people together under a common belief in Christ, stating that Christ is the ultimate authority, whose influence extends beyond any borders or boundaries, and that everyone is accountable to him.

Though the feast is relatively new, the theology underlying the feast is as ancient as the Church and as profound as the mystery of our faith. By his life, death, and resurrection Jesus opened the path to salvation for all of us. By virtue of our baptism, we are placed on this path toward salvation, with Jesus Christ as our supreme guide.

Depictions of Christ the King, or Christ in Majesty, show Christ seated on a royal throne, often clad in blue and red. Blue is a heavenly color, referencing Christ's divinity, and red is the color of Jesus' passion and death, referencing his humanity. He often wears the regalia typical of a king: the crown on his head, the scepter in his right hand, and the *globus cruciger*, or the orb crowned with a cross, in his left hand.

The crown and scepter indicate royal power, and the globe with the cross is of particular interest. The image of a ruler holding an orb suggests that the ruler holds the world in his hand. Roman emperors were depicted with this orb. When Christianity became an accepted religion of the Roman Empire, Christian emperors added a cross to the orb, indicating that they were governing the world for God. When the *globus cruciger* is placed in Christ's hands, it indicates that Christ is the ruler of the universe as well as the *Salvator Mundi*, or Savior of the World. Borrowing from earthly regal symbology, Christ is depicted both as the Savior of the World and as the one who rules over the world and who, at the end of time, will be the judge of all.

The Sacred Heart of Jesus

Devotion to the Sacred Heart is rooted in a deep gratitude for the love Christ extends to all of us, even unto death on the cross. Early devotion to this selfless love was focused on the side of Jesus that was pierced while he hung on the cross. Over time, this boundless love of Christ became associated with his heart. Private devotions to the Heart of Jesus started to emerge around the tenth century and became very popular in religious communities between the thirteenth and sixteenth centuries.

Public devotions to the Sacred Heart of Jesus evolved in response to the visions of Sister Mary Margaret Alacoque, a Visitation sister who lived in the seventeenth century. In her visions, Jesus spoke of his love for the people and his disappointment about the lack of love that he received in return. He called for a feast that would celebrate his love and repair the lack of love he saw demonstrated. As a result of Sr. Mary Margaret's visions, the feast of the Sacred Heart of Jesus was founded and celebrated locally, especially in France. In 1856, Pope Pius IX declared that the feast of the Sacred Heart of Jesus was to be celebrated by the entire Church on the Friday after the solemnity of the Body and Blood of Christ. The feast was elevated to the rank of a solemnity after the Second Vatican Council and continues to be celebrated on the Friday after the solemnity of the Body and Blood of Christ.

The image of the Sacred Heart shows Jesus presenting his heart to us. It is a heart on fire with love for the people. It is topped with a crown of thorns, which reminds us of Jesus' sacrificial love and the fact that he loves us so deeply that he was willing to die for us. This imagery expresses Jesus' love for us, calls us to a profound sense of gratitude, and invites us to share in his sacrificial love for God's people. Like Jesus, we are asked to love without condition.

The Divine Mercy

Saint Faustina, a member of the Congregation of Our Lady of Mercy, had many visions of Jesus, the Blessed Mother, heaven, hell, and purgatory. In 1930, Jesus appeared to her dressed in a white garment, with red and pale blue rays emanating from his heart. According to her diary, Jesus described the colors as follows: "The pale ray stands for the water, which makes souls righteous. The red ray stands for the blood, which is the life of souls.... These two rays issued forth from the very depths of my tender mercy when My agonized heart was opened by a lance on the cross."

Thus, the blue represents baptism, the sacrament by which we are cleansed from all sin, including original sin. The red represents Jesus's sacrifice on the cross, by which we have been saved.

According to St. Faustina's diary, Jesus asked her to paint an image of him as he had appeared to her. He went on to say that he desired for this image to be venerated throughout the world, especially on the second Sunday of Easter, which was to be known as the feast of Divine Mercy.

The first version of the Divine Mercy, based on St. Faustina's description, was painted by Eugene Kazimierowski in 1934. On the second Sunday of Easter in 1935, it was venerated for the first time. Since then, many versions of the Divine Mercy have been painted. The constant elements are the white robe, the blue and red

rays, and the dynamism of the painting as Jesus steps forward while raising his right hand in a blessing. Some versions show the wounds on Jesus' hands and feet.

Saint Faustina died in 1938 from tuberculosis. She was beatified by Pope St. John Paul II in 1993 and was canonized by him in 2000. Her feast day is October 5. During her canonization, Pope St. John Paul II designated the second Sunday of Easter as Divine Mercy Sunday. Since then, devotion to the Divine Mercy has become very popular, and the depictions are widespread.

Depictions of the Blessed Virgin Mary

The oldest images we have of the Blessed Mother date back to the late third and early fourth centuries and can be found in Roman catacombs. Since these humble beginnings, representations of Mary have become innumerable and very diverse. They are found in most every cathedral, church, and chapel as well as in our homes. Statues of Mary have been created in wood, bronze, stone, and plaster. Her image is embroidered on banners, tapestries, and chasubles and is portrayed in paintings, frescos, stained-glass windows, and mosaics.

Most numerous are the many versions of the image of Mother and Child. In addition, specific moments in the life of Mary as they are described in the gospels, such as the annunciation and the visitation, have inspired many artists. Other images affirm theological truths about Mary, such as the depictions of the immaculate conception or the assumption of Mary into heaven. Still others remember and celebrate specific apparitions of Mary, such as Our Lady of Lourdes and Our Lady of Guadalupe. Representations of Our Lady of the Immaculate Conception, Our Lady of Czestochowa, and Our Lady of Guadalupe are among those most commonly seen, and they are but a small representation of the many ways that our Blessed Mother has shown her infinite care for humanity as the Mother of God.

Our Lady of the Immaculate Conception

Our Lady of the Immaculate Conception is a very popular depiction of Mary. The doctrine of the immaculate conception holds that Mary was born without personal or original sin. The word "immaculate" is a contraction of two Latin words: *in*, meaning "not" or "opposite of," and *maculatus*, meaning "spotted or defiled," from *macula*, meaning "spot or blemish." The dogma of the immaculate conception was pronounced in 1854 by Pope Pius IX. However, the devotion to and depictions of Our Lady of the Immaculate Conception pre-date this dogma by several centuries.

Details in the depiction of Our Lady of the Immaculate Conception may differ from image to image, but most renditions show Mary standing on the moon and crowned with twelve stars, as referenced in the Book of Revelation: "A great sign appeared in the sky, a woman clothed with the sun, with the moon under her feet, and on her head a crown of twelve stars" (Revelation 12:1).

A popular addition to the imagery is the serpent trampled by Mary's foot. The serpent refers to the original sin that came into the world through the cunning of the snake and the disobedience of Adam and Eve. Mary, as the new Eve, crushes the snake because she will give birth to the Savior, Jesus, the new Adam who will reopen the gates to heaven that had been closed to all.

In 1847, Our Lady of the Immaculate Conception was declared the patron saint of the United States of America. Devotion increased substantially in 1858, after the apparition of Mary to Bernadette Soubirous, a young French girl to whom Mary revealed her identity by saying, "I am the Immaculate Conception." This encounter led to the famous Our Lady of Lourdes grotto and many miraculous healings associated with prayer to Our Lady of the Immaculate Conception. Her feast is celebrated on December 8 and is a holy day of obligation in the United States.

Our Lady of Czestochowa

The image of our Lady of Czestochowa is recognizable by the fact that the faces of mother and child are black, and there is a double scar on Mary's right cheek. She is also known as the Black Madonna of Czestochowa.

The history of this icon is very complex and wrapped in mystery. Some people say it was actually painted by Saint Luke and handed down through history. What is certain is that this icon has been in Czestochowa, Poland, since 1381.

The black color is the result of a fire that occurred in the church where the painting hung. Our Lady of Czestochowa is credited with having saved the church from complete destruction by this fire. The scars on her face are said to have been inflicted on the image when the church was robbed by thieves. When the looters tried to flee with the church's treasures, their horses refused to move. In anger, they threw the image of Our Lady onto the floor and stabbed her several times. Some versions of the story say that the image started to bleed. Others say that the robber who inflicted the wounds fell to the ground and died when he attempted a third slash. Early attempts to restore the painting failed, and even today the faces are blackened and the scars are present.

Our Lady of Czestochowa was declared the queen and protector of Poland in 1656. Today, her shrine remains the most popular shrine in Poland. She is also revered by people of Polish descent throughout the world.

Our Lady of Guadalupe

Throughout Christian history, Mary has appeared in almost every part of the world to encourage people, give them hope, or call them to more holy lives. In nearly every one of those instances, she presented herself in the image of the people to whom she appeared.

The most popular apparition in the Americas is Our Lady of Guadalupe. She appeared in Tepeyac, near Mexico City, as an Aztec princess to Juan Diego, a local peasant, in 1531. When Juan Diego's bishop asked for proof of her appearance, Our Lady showed Juan Diego a rosebush that was blooming in winter. She told him to wrap the red roses in his mantle, or poncho, and bring them to the bishop. When he opened his mantle to show the roses to the bishop, an exact image of the beautiful Lady who had appeared to Juan Diego was on the mantle. This mantle, which was made from fragile yucca fiber, is still preserved and on display, with the image intact, at the Basilica of Our Lady of Guadalupe in Mexico City.

The image is truly rich in symbology, as it presents Mary as the Virgin Mother of God. Her posture in general is very similar to that of Our Lady of the Immaculate Conception: one foot forward, hands folded devoutly, and gazing benevolently at the people.

The rays of the sun around Our Lady and the moon at her feet are a reference to the second chapter of Revelation, in which Mary is described as "the woman clothed with the sun with the moon under her feet" and clad with

stars on her mantle. Some people suggest that the stars are shown as the constellation above Tepeyac on December 12, 1531, the day Our Lady appeared to Juan Diego.

The angel at the bottom of the image appears to be carrying Our Lady. This is not unusual in Marian iconography, as angels or putti are often shown carrying Mary especially, in representations of her assumption. In Aztec culture, only people of royal descent were carried on the shoulders by others. The angel carrying Mary affirms that she is the Queen of Heaven.

The mantle Our Lady is wearing is turquoise. In Aztec culture, turquoise was the color of the gods and of royalty. Thus, Our Lady appears as royalty, for she is the Queen of Heaven and the Mother of God. The gold trim on her mantle confirms that she is royalty. The sash Our Lady is wearing is black and is worn high above her waist. This is what Aztec aristocratic women did when they were pregnant. This suggests that Our Lady is pregnant with the Son of God.

In 1754, Pope Benedict XIV declared Our Lady of Guadalupe the patroness of "new Spain." She was declared the patroness of the Americas by Pope St. John Paul II in 1999. Many churches in Mexico and the United States host an image or a shrine of Our Lady of Guadalupe. Her feast is celebrated on December 12.

Our Lady of La Vang

The persecution of Vietnamese Catholics began in 1798. Many of them hid in the forest of La Vang. At night, they gathered in small groups to pray the rosary. One night, Our Lady appeared to them in their own image, dressed in traditional Vietnamese garb. She held the Baby Jesus in her arms, while two angels appeared at her side. She consoled the people and gave them some advice, including about the usage of medicinal plants. She continued to appear throughout the persecution, which lasted almost a century.

In 1886, after the persecution ended, Our Lady of La Vang was declared the protector of the Catholics in Vietnam, and a church was built in her honor. This church was declared a National Marian Shrine by the Vietnamese bishops in 1961. The next year, Pope St. John XXIII elevated the church of La Vang to the status of minor basilica. Pope St. John Paul II affirmed the great importance of Our Lady of La Vang and encouraged continued devotion to her during the canonization of 117 Vietnamese martyrs on June 19, 1988.

Images of Our Lady of La Vang depict her with Eurasian features, and she is wearing the traditional Vietnamese áo dài flowing dress and the typical khăn đống crescent-shaped hat. She holds the Baby Jesus, who raises his right hand in the traditional blessing. Her feast is celebrated on November 22.

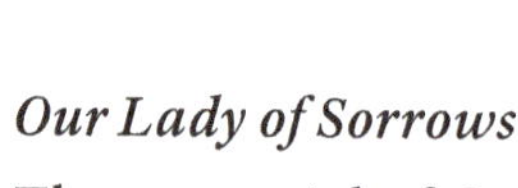

Our Lady of Sorrows

The memorial of Our Lady of Sorrows is, befittingly, September 15, the day after the feast of the Exaltation of the Cross. The history of this memorial is complex. Before the revision of the liturgical calendar following the Second Vatican Council, two days were dedicated to Our Lady of Sorrows, each with its own rich history: one on the Friday before Palm Sunday, which is the older of the two, and one on the third Sunday in September. The new calendar merged both into the September 15 memorial.

There has been a long-standing Catholic devotion to the suffering of Mary in general and the Seven Sorrows of Mary in particular. The seven sorrows include:

- The prophecy of Simeon
- The flight into Egypt
- The loss of the Child Jesus in the Temple of Jerusalem
- Mary meeting Jesus on the Via Dolorosa (not found in the New Testament)
- Jesus' crucifixion
- Jesus being taken down from the cross
- Jesus' burial by Joseph of Arimathea

Our Lady of Sorrows has been a popular subject in devotional art for both private and public use. In these images, Mary is often depicted with seven swords piercing her heart, which is a reference to both the prophecy of Simeon (See Luke 2:25–35.) that a sword would pierce Mary's heart and the aforementioned Seven Sorrows of Mary. Sometimes, only one sword pierces her heart. Grand processions with the statue of Our Lady of Sorrows on an elaborate float are very popular in many countries as part of the Holy Week observance.

Our Lady, Undoer of Knots

Devotion to Our Lady, Undoer of Knots originated in Bavaria at the beginning of the eighteenth century. While Pope Francis was spending time in Germany as a student, he discovered this devotion and loved it. He brought it back with him to Argentina, where it quickly became popular. When Francis was elected pope, this devotion became popular around the world.

The original image of Our Lady, Undoer of Knots was commissioned by a Bavarian priest, Fr. Langenmantel, to celebrate that Our Lady had saved the marriage of his grandfather, Wolfgang Langenmantel. When Wolfgang Langenmantel and his wife, Sophia, were on the verge of divorce, Wolfgang sought the advice of Fr. Jakob Rem, a local Jesuit priest. Wolfgang met with Fr. Rem four times. For the last visit, Fr. Rem asked Wolfgang to bring his wedding ribbon. At that time, it was customary to tie a ribbon around the couple's hands during their wedding after the vows and exchange of rings.

Fr. Rem took the ribbon and held it while praying before an image of Our Lady of the Snows. Then Fr. Rem turned around and solemnly untied the wedding knot, smoothing out the ribbon. As he was doing that, the ribbon started to glow and became intensely white. Wolfgang felt that this symbolized Our Lady solving his marital problems, and he returned to his wife.

The first image of Our Lady, Undoer of Knots depicts Mary suspended between heaven and earth, suggesting that she is the one who mediates between us and God. The Holy Spirit, under the typical form of a dove, hovers above her, affirming that it was by the Holy Spirit that she became the Mother of God. She is standing on the moon, a snake circling her feet, which is a reference to the Immaculate Conception.

The snake is coiled in a knot. This is a visual confirmation that all the knots or difficulties we experience as humans have their origin in the snake that tempted Adam and Eve to eat the forbidden fruit.

An angel to Mary's left presents a rope with numerous knots, which Mary unties one by one. An angel on her right presents the rope, free of knots. At the bottom of the painting is an angel leading a man to Mary. There are two interpretations for this. First, it could be a reference to the Book of Tobit, in which the Archangel Rafael accompanied Tobias on his journey to Medina. A second interpretation is that this is Wolfgang Langenmantel being led to Mary. Several variations on this original painting have been created.

Depictions of the Saints

Each one of our saints is recognizable by their own symbol, or attribute, that helps us identify them. Saint Peter is often shown holding a set of keys. This is a reference to Jesus' words to Peter: "I will give you the keys to the kingdom of heaven. Whatever you bind on earth shall be bound in heaven; and whatever you loose on earth shall be loosed in heaven" (Matthew 16:19). This, in turn, is rooted in the promise God made to Eliakim: "I will place the key of the House of David on his shoulder; what he opens, no one will shut, what he shuts, no one will open" (Isaiah 22:22), thus bestowing all power on him. Another example is Saint Clare of Assisi, who is sometimes shown holding a monstrance, which is reminiscent of when she defended her monastery while holding a monstrance that warded off the enemy. Knowledge of the lives of the saints helps us interpret these symbols, known as attributes, and identify the saints.

Saint Joseph

One of the most popular saints, next to the Blessed Mother, is St. Joseph. He is usually depicted as holding a child with his left arm and a blooming staff with lilies in his right hand. The baby, of course is Jesus, the foster child of St. Joseph. The meaning of the lilies is a bit more complicated. A popular explanation is that the lily is a symbol of chastity, as we honor Joseph as the most-chaste spouse of Mary, the Mother of Jesus. The older interpretation is based on the Gospel of Pseudo-Matthew and the Pro-to-Gospel of James, neither of which are part of the Bible. Because these texts have a lot of details about Mary's life and Jesus' childhood that are not mentioned in the gospels, they became quite popular and filled in the gaps.

In these texts is a description of how Joseph came to be selected as the spouse for Mary. Eligible bachelors were invited to bring their staffs to the temple and place them on the altar. When Joseph placed his staff on the altar, the Holy Spirit, under the form of a dove, descended on it, thus indicating that he was to be betrothed to Mary. These texts and many others inspired the mid-thirteenth-century Golden Legend, or *Legenda Aurea*, which is a collection of accounts of the lives of the saints. The account in the Golden Legend of the selection of Mary's spouse happened in a similar way. Eligible bachelors were to place their staffs on the altar in the temple and were told "One of these branches will bloom, and the Holy Spirit in the form of a dove will perch upon its tip, according to the prophecy of Isaiah. The man to whom this branch belongs is, beyond all doubt, the one who is to be the virgin's spouse."

According to the Golden Legend, St. Joseph thought himself too old to become the husband of the Virgin Mary, so he stood back while the others placed their staffs on the altar. But nothing happened. Then, the Divine voice declared "that the only man who had not brought his branch was the one to whom the virgin was to be espoused. Therefore, St. Joseph brought his branch forward, it flowered at once, and a dove came from heaven and perched upon it. So, it was clear to all that Joseph was to be Mary's husband." Ever since, Joseph has been depicted carrying a blooming staff.

The Apostles

All the apostles—except for John the Beloved, also known as John the Theologian—died as martyrs for the faith. Saint John was sent in exile to the Island of Patmos, where he died at an old age. Because they died for the faith, the apostles are often depicted holding a Bible in addition to the instrument of their martyrdom.

Saint Andrew, the brother of St. Peter, was crucified on a saltire, or X-shaped cross. Therefore, he is often depicted holding an X-shaped cross. He considered himself unworthy to be crucified in the same manner as Jesus and therefore asked for a saltire. **Saint Bartholomew,** who was flayed alive, is depicted with a knife and often has his skin draped over his arm. **Saint Simon,** known as the Zealot, is often holding a saw, the tool of his martyrdom. **Saint Matthew,** who was martyred by the sword, is often shown carrying a sword. Since he is identified as the author of one of the gospels, he may hold a book, and because he was a tax collector, he sometimes is depicted with bags of money. **Saint Thomas,** who doubted the resurrection and preached the gospel in India, is believed to have been martyred there with a spear, which he carries as his attribute in many depictions. **Saint Matthias,** who was chosen to replace Judas, the one who betrayed Jesus, is identifiable by a battle-axe, the tool of his martyrdom. **Saint Philip** was crucified on a Latin cross, the same type used for Jesus. In addition to a cross, he sometimes holds a basket of bread, which is a reference to his

in the aforementioned tetramorph. He sometimes holds a cup with a snake, which refers to an exchange he had with a pagan priest who said he would convert to Christianity if St. John drank from a cup with poison. Saint John prayed over the cup, and the poison, in the form of a snake, left the cup before he drank from it.

The most frequently used attributes to identify **Saint Peter** are a set of two oversized keys and an upside-down cross. The keys refer to a passage in the Gospel of Matthew where Jesus says: "I will give you the keys to the kingdom of heaven. Whatever you bind on earth shall be bound in heaven; and whatever you loose on earth shall be loosed in heaven" (Matthew 16:19). The cross is upside down because, like Andrew, Peter did not think himself worthy to be crucified in the same manner as Jesus. A very famous statue of St. Peter in St. Peter's Basilica in the Vatican depicts him seated on a throne and dressed in papal attire, including the triple-crowned papal tiara, thus affirming that the pope is the successor of St. Peter, the first pope.

questioning how one basket of bread would feed 5,000. (See John 6:1–15.) **Saint James the Lesser** is commonly depicted with a club, associated with his martyrdom. Sometimes, he holds a scroll. This is interpreted by some as a reference to the Apostles' Creed. Though this version of the Creed is associated with the apostles, there is no explicit evidence that he is the author. **Saint Jude** holds a club, an axe, or a spear, all symbolizing his martyrdom. The book he holds is a reference to the Letter of Jude in the New Testament.

Saint John is often shown with a book and a quill, as he is the author of the fourth gospel. Other attributes are an eagle, as he is the eagle

Saint James, the son of Zebedee, also known as **Saint James the Greater,** is believed to be buried in Santiago de Compostela. The name of the town is directly related to this saint, as "Santiago" is a contraction of *santi* ("saint") and *Iago* ("James.") According to tradition, his burial site was miraculously found when a hermit saw a shower of stars over a field. Compostela is based on the Latin *campus* *stellae*, which means "field of stars." Santiago de Compostela became one of the premier places of pilgrimage in the Middle Ages, and St. James became the patron saint of pilgrims. Because of that, he is often depicted with a staff to support him during the journey and a shell to scoop water from a stream.

Saint Paul: Apostle to the Gentiles

Though, strictly speaking, not one of the apostles, St. Paul is often referred to as the "Apostle to the Gentiles" because he traveled throughout the entire Roman Empire to proclaim the Good News. Most representations of St. Paul show him holding a sword in one hand and a book in the other. The sword refers to his martyrdom by the sword in 64 AD. The book represents the letters he wrote to the many communities he visited, which are now part of the New Testament. Saint Paul is often paired with St. Peter as the foundational pillars of the Church. Saint Peter is the "rock" upon which the Church was built (See Matthew 16:18.), whereas St. Paul exemplifies the missionary zeal of the Church.

Saint Mary of Magdala: Apostle to the Apostles

For centuries, the Catholic Church identified Mary of Magdala with the repentant sinner who anointed Jesus' feet. (See Luke 7:36–50.) Pope Gregory the Great (590–604) affirmed this in a homily in which he identified Mary of Magdala with the sinful yet unnamed woman who washed Jesus' feet. This was based on two other Scripture passages in which Mary of Magdala was healed by Jesus of seven demons (Luke 8:1–3 and Mark 16:9). These demons were believed to be the seven deadly sins, with lust being one of them. In addition, Mary of Magdala was also thought to be the unnamed adulteress who was saved by Jesus from stoning. (See John 8:3–11.)

Recent scholarship holds that there is no proof that Mary of Magdala was the woman who washed Jesus' feet or the woman who was about to be stoned. Even the identification of the seven demons with the seven deadly sins is questioned. Today, it is believed that Mary of Magdala was an independently wealthy woman who supported Jesus in his mission (See Luke 8:1–2.) and who was the first witness to the resurrection. In 2016, Pope Francis elevated the memorial of Mary of Magdala to a feast, which is the same status as that of most apostles. Her title as repentant sinner was superseded by *apostolum apostola*, or "Apostle to the Apostles." This "new" title has been commonly used in the Eastern Church and was also a title given to her by St. Thomas Aquinas.

The most popular depiction of Mary of Magdala is at the foot of the cross at the time of Jesus' crucifixion. Alluding to her status as the repentant prostitute, she is always depicted with long flowing hair, which sets her apart from proper women who had their hair covered. Two symbols, or attributes, are associated with Mary of Magdala: a flagon with myrrh and a red egg.

The myrrh, of course, is a reference to the fact that she was one of the women returning to Jesus' tomb after the Sabbath to anoint his body. The red egg is a bit more complicated, as there are several different narratives. The most popular is that Mary of Magdala joined Sts. Peter and Paul in their missionary efforts, even finagling an invitation to a dinner at the Roman imperial court, where she professed her faith in the resurrection. Emperor Tiberius did not believe her and handed her an egg, saying that Jesus rising from the dead was as likely as the egg turning red. Before he finished speaking, the egg turned a bright red, and she continued proclaiming the gospel to the entire imperial house.

Throughout her life, Mary of Magdala continued to preach the gospel. As she grew older, she is said to have retired to Ephesus, where she lived with Mary, the mother of Jesus, and John, the beloved disciple. Her feast is celebrated on July 22.

Faithful Reflections

Our churches are filled with images that speak about our faith, serve as testimonies to our Christian history, and honor the saints who led the way with their faith, their lives, and sometimes martyrdom. However, much of this witness is no longer recognized or understood because the meaning of the imagery has been lost, forgotten, or distorted.

Set aside some time to walk around your church and look for images that you might have walked by every day and not realized were there. Look to the altar for images that speak of sacrifice and Christ's selfless love. Look to the area of proclamation or the *Gospel Book* to find expressions of the holy apostles who recorded the testimonies of those who encountered Jesus' teaching and took on the task of passing them down to the generations to follow. We all share that task and are called to pass on the stories of our faith by understanding and explaining the meaning of the symbols that are alive within the Mass and beyond. Knowledge of our faith is a wonderful gift. How will you pass on your gift to others?

- *Discover the monograms or acronyms present in your church. Learn why they are located where they are and share their meaning with someone.*
- *Identify the statues of saints in your church that you do not already know. Find their visual attributes, such as St. Joseph's lily, and research what they mean. Read about their lives and identify one way that you can learn and grow from their witness.*
- *What Christian symbol is most powerful for you? Reflect on that symbol and how it can support you on your journey of faith.*

List of Images and Image Credits

Page 4
Stained glass window detail of the Virgin Saint Mary
Shutterstock / Sky Light Pictures

Page 6
Crucifix with rose window
Ken Fournelle

Page 8
The Lamb of God, mosaic
Shutterstock / Zvonimir Atletic

Page 10
Woman holding a photograph
Pexels / Ivan Samkov

Page 12
Receiving the Eucharist
Ken Fournelle

Page 14
Easter Vigil, Basilica of Saint Mary, Minneapolis, Minnesota
Mike Jensen

Page 16
Man in prayer
Cathopic / Lupe Belmonte

Page 17
Traffic light
Shutterstock /Binkski

Page 18
Baptism
Shutterstock / sweet marshmallow

Page 19
Wedding rings
Pexels / Caio

Page 20
Confirmation
Cathopic / mattkolf

Page 21
Holy Spirit, fresco
Cathopic / Diego Andrés Esquivel Pereira

Page 24
Woman carrying water
Ken Fournelle

Page 24
Baptism vessel
Cathopic / Amy Stout

Page 27
Blessing with holy water at the Basilica of Saint Mary,
Minneapolis, Minnesota
Ken Fournelle

Page 28
Easter fire
Mike Jensen

Page 29
Presentation of the holy oils, Basilica of Saint Mary,
Minneapolis, Minnesota
Ken Fournelle

Page 30
Oil of holy chrism
Cathopic / Daniel Razniewski

Page 31
Chalice with wine and bread
Shutterstock / Magdalena Kucova

Page 32
Miracle of the Bread and Fish, Giovanni Lanfranco
Wikimedia Commons

Page 33
Eucharist
Shutterstock / wideonet

Page 36
Brussels Cathedral
Need source

Page 38
Sunset over Saint Peter's Square, Vatican
Shutterstock / AlexKnyaz

Page 39
Piedroits, or column statues, of north portal (12th c.),
Cathedral of Saint Denis, Paris
Wikimedia Commons

Page 40
Parish choir
Cathopic

Page 41
Palm Sunday procession
Mike Jensen

Page 42
Baptistery, Florence, Italy
Johan van Parys

Page 43
Adult baptism
Ken Fournelle

Page 44
Baptismal font
Johan van Parys

Page 45
Dove container for the Eucharist, Bethany Chapel of the
Archdiocese of Boston Pastoral Center

Page 46
Sanctuary light and tabernacle
Source needed

Page 47
Reconciliation room
Johan van Parys

Page 48
Sacristy
Cathopic / Lupe Belmonte

Page 50
The Last Supper (wood carving), Sr. Mary Ann Osborne, SSND
Johan van Parys

Page 52
Our Lady of Tenderness, Deb Korluka
Johan van Parys

Page 54
Nuestra Senora del Carmen, Gabriel Vigil, private collection
Johan van Parys

Page 55
Jesus Meets His Mother, fourth Station of the Cross
Hohenberg, Germany
Shutterstock / Zvonimir Atletic

Page 56
African crucifix
Johan van Parys

Page 57
Milagro display, Naples, Italy
Shutterstock / lindasky76

Page 58
Frederick Hart, *Cross of the Millennium* (1/3 life-size), clear acrylic resin, 1992, © Chesley LLC
Mike Jensen

Page 59
Our Lady of Africa
Denise Anderson

Page 60
The Last Supper, Leonardo Da Vinci
Wikimedia Commons

Page 61
Angels Unawares, Timothy Schmalz, St. Peter's Square, Vatican City
Johan van Parys

Page 62
Altar in a chapel
Cathopic / @malenymedina

Page 63
Sanctuary in Chimayo, New Mexico
Johan van Parys

Page 64
Veronica Wipes the Face of Jesus, sixth Station of the Cross
Cathopic / Javier Bastidas

Page 65
Statue of Saint Joan of Arc (19th c.)
Cathopic / Joan Sutter

Page 66
Our Lady of Good Counsel, Vatican Mosaic Studios
Johan van Parys

Page 68
Baptismal font, Saint Mary's Cathedral, Sydney, Australia
Johan van Parys

Page 70
Altar, Saint James Cathedral, Seattle, Washington
Johan van Parys

Page 70
Ambo, Santa Maria de la Paz, Santa Fe, New Mexico-
Johan van Parys

Page 71
Covered baptismal font, Cathedral Basilica, St. Louis, Missouri
Denise Anderson

Page72
Saint Mary of the Lake, Alexandria, Minnesota
Johan van Parys

Page 73
Bishop's chair, Saint James Cathedral, Orlando, Florida
Johan van Parys

Page 74
Tabernacle
Cathopic / Rita Laura Miño

Page 75
Paschal lamb on tabernacle door, Provence, France
Johan van Parys

Page 76
Crucifix
Cathopic / Frames Cristianos

Page 78
Thurible
Shutterstock / Ander Aguirre

Page 80
Processional cross
Cathopic / *Jornada Mundial de la Juventud*

Page 81
Processional cross, Debra Korluka,
Basilica of Saint Mary, Minneapolis, Minnesota
Johan van Parys

Page 82
Paschal candle
Shutterstock / Francisco Amaral Leitao

Page 115
Farewell of Saints Peter and Paul, Alonzo Rodriguez (16th c.)
Wikimedia Commons

Page 116
Commingling
Denise Anderson

Page 117
Woman kneeling in prayer
Mike Jensen

Page 118
A person prays in silence
Mike Jensend

Page 119
Distribution of ashes
Dave Hrbacek

Page 120
Distribution of ashes
Ken Fournelle

Page 122
Advent wreath, Basilica of Saint Mary, Minneapolis, Minnesota
Johan van Parys

Page 124
Advent wreath
Shutterstock / horizonphoto

Page 125
Altar adorned for Christmas
Need source

Page 126
Nativity scene
Cathopic / Coffee With Damian

Page 127
The passing of the cross, Basilica of Saint Mary, Minneapolis, Minnesota
Mike Jensen

Page 128
Open tabernacle, Saint Thomas More, St. Paul, Minnesota
Denise Anderson

Page 129
Pope Francis at an Easter Vigil service, Vatican
Catholic News Agency / Daniel Ibanez

Page 130
Easter cross
Shutterstock / Chad Zuber

Page 132
Christ on the Cold Stone, Saint Savior Cathedral, Bruges, Belgium

Page 134
IHS
Johan van Parys

Page 134
Monogram of Christ on a plaque of a sarcophagus (4th c.)
Wikimedia Commons

Page 135
Crucifix

Page 135
IXOYE
Johan van Parys

Page 136
Altar with pelican mosaic
Denise Anderson

Page 137
Tetramorph carving decorating the altar at the Shrine of the Little Flower, Albuquerque, New Mexico:
Gospel of Matthew
Gospel of Mark
Gospel of Luke
Gospel of John
Denise Anderson

Page 138
Jesus as the Good Shepherd, fresco (3rd c.)
Wikimedia Commons

Page 139
Jesus Christ as Pantocrator, from the Deësis mosaic in the Hagia Sophia, Istanbul (late 13th c.)
Wikimedia Commons

Page 140
Christ in Majesty, Thomas Gaytee Glass Studio, Basilica of Saint Mary, Minneapolis, Minnesota
Mike Jensen

Page 141
The Sacred Heart of Jesus, Basilica of Saint Mary, Minneapolis, Minnesota
Johan van Parys

Page 142
Divine Mercy, Eugeniusz Kazimirowski (1934)
Wikimedia Commons

Page 143
The earliest fresco of the Virgin Mary, Catacomb of Priscilla (early 3rd c.)
Wikimedia Commons

Page 144
Our Lady of Częstochowa
Denise Anderson

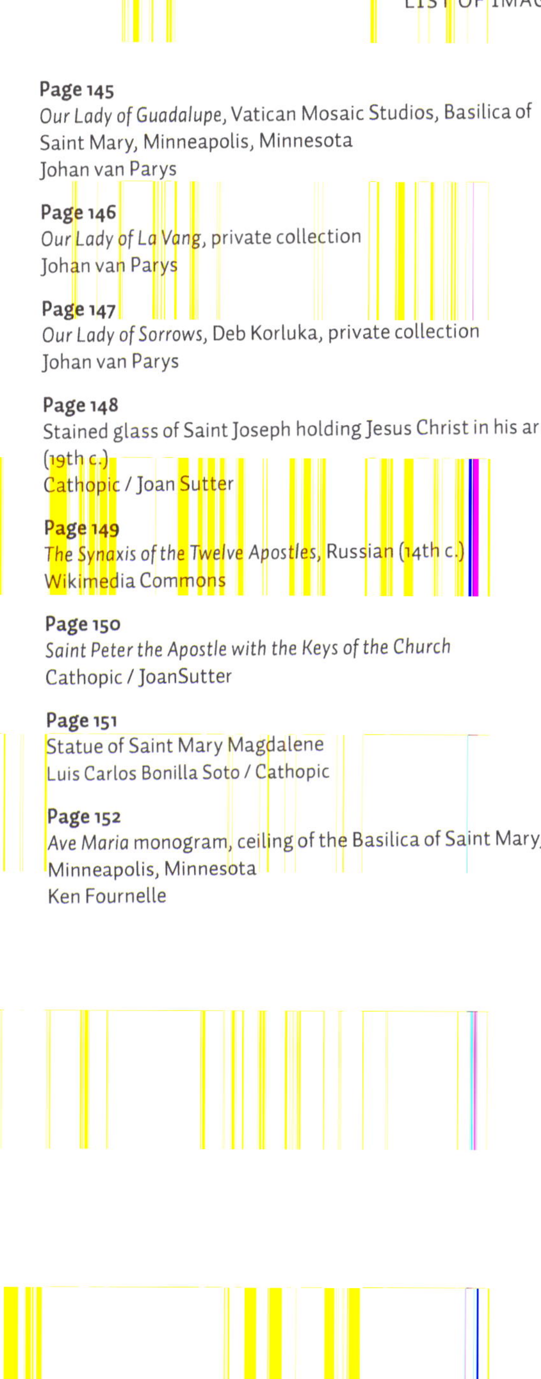

About the Author

Johan van Parys is the director of liturgy and sacred arts at the Basilica of Saint Mary in Minneapolis. He also teaches liturgy in the School of Theology of St. John's University and is the co-founder and president of the Minnesota/North Dakota chapter of the Patrons of the Arts in the Vatican Museums. Dr. van Parys received his doctorate in theology in liturgical studies from the University of Notre Dame and has graduate degrees from the Catholic University of Louvain, Belgium, in archeology, art history, architecture, and religious studies.

www.ingramcontent.com/pod-product-compliance
Lightning Source LLC
Chambersburg PA
BHW040259230126
5CB00006BA/18

9 7 8 0 7 6 4 8 2 8 8 5 0 *